The Power of Natural Healing

THE POWER OF
NATURAL HEALING

by
Hua-Ching Ni

SEVEN STAR
COMMUNICATIONS

SANTA MONICA

The College of Tao offers teachings about health, spirituality and the Integral Way based on the teachings of Hua-Ching Ni. To obtain information about the Integral Way of Life Correspondence Course, please write the College of Tao, PO Box 1222, El Prado, NM 87529 USA. To obtain information about Mentors teaching in your area or country, please write the Universal Society of the Integral Way, PO Box 28993, Atlanta, GA 30358-0993 USA.

Acknowledgment: Thanks and appreciation to all students who assisted with this book.

Published by:
Seven Star Communications Group Inc.
1314 Second Street
Santa Monica, CA 90401 USA

The paper used in this publication meets the minimum requirements of the American National Standard for Information Sciences Permanence of Paper for Printed Library Materials, ANSI 239.48-1984.

First Printing February 1991
Second Printing September 1995

Library of Congress Cataloging-in-Publication Data
Ni, Hua Ching.
    The power of natural healing / by Ni, Hua-Ching.
      p. cm.
    Includes index.
    .ISBN 0-937064-31-9 (pbk.)
      1. Taoism. 2. Spiritual life--Taoism. I. Title.
    BL1924.N483 1990   90-60823
    299'.5142--dc20   CIP

This book is dedicated
to those who will find their true savior
within their lives.

To all readers,

According to the teaching of the Universal Integral Way, male and female are equally important in the natural sphere. This fact is confirmed in the diagram of *T'ai Chi*. Thus, discrimination is not practiced in our tradition. All of my work is dedicated to both genders of the human race.

Wherever possible, constructions using masculine pronouns to represent both sexes are avoided. Where they occur, we ask your tolerance and spiritual understanding. We hope that you will take the essence of my teaching and overlook the limitations of language. Gender discrimination is inherent in English. Ancient Chinese pronouns do not differentiate gender. I wish that all of you will achieve yourselves well above the level of language and gender.

Thank you, H. C. Ni

Contents

The Universal Way

The Universal Way is the destination
  of all spiritual efforts of humankind.
It serves all people's lives,
  everywhere and always.
The Universal Way conveys the deep truth
  of all conscious elaborations of the human mind.
It contains the vast and profound essence
  of the human spirit.
Thus it transcends all religious teachings,
  leaving them behind,
  like the clothing of a bygone season.
The Universal Way is the goal of all sciences,
  but is not locked at the level of the intellect.
It cuts through all wasteful skepticism
  and inexhaustible searching.
Thus it surpasses all sciences,
  leaving them behind
  like historical relics of the past.
The Subtle Essence that is sought
  by all sciences and all religions
  transcends all attempts to reach it
  by means of thought, belief or experiment.
The Universal Way leads directly to it
  and guides you to reach it yourself
  by uniting with the Integral Nature of the Universe.
The Universal Way is like the master key
  to all doors leading to the inner room
  of ultimate truth.
It is the master teaching of all teachings,
  yet it relies on no religions and no experiments.
There is no need for intellectual or emotional detours
  that cannot serve the lives of all people
  everywhere and always.
Follow the Universal Way beyond all boundaries
  to the heart and essence of natural life itself.

Preface

I

The earliest faith of humankind was the faith in natural vitality. Throughout the span of human life on this planet, people have always relied on the constancy of nature, knowing that although night comes, day will dawn again, and that when winter comes, spring is not far behind. Even when winter was longer than usual, spring always came. Many generations of a trustworthy relationship with nature forged a natural faith in universal vitality, which came to be called Tao, or the constant path of universal nature. The word Tao later came to include the routine changes of human society and history. Thus, Tao also represented the law of human society and individual life. By following it, people experienced health and prosperity; by ignoring it they encountered trouble and difficulty.

Tao, in its three aspects of nature, society and the individual could be called a nonverbal elasticity or subtle law that governs the rhythm and changes of all things. Its workings can be foretold by people who have cultivated their own spiritual sensitivity to a high degree.

Spiritual sensitivity can also help a person avoid making mistakes that would trouble or damage his life. By gathering subtle information from the environment and by following basic disciplines and practices that utilize natural sources of energy such as sunlight, moonlight, starlight, water, air and natural herbs, a person can prevent danger or make necessary psychological adjustments to unavoidable difficulty. Those who knew how to make use of such resources lived longer than other people and eventually came to be regarded as "immortals."

Since people have become more conceptually developed, they have also become more confused and need to learn some simple ancient wisdom to improve their lives. This book, which focuses on natural vitality and healing, can help people develop clarity at all levels of their lives.

II

Originally, people did not have a concept or image of a powerful, ruling god. That image is a cultural product of the last 3,000 years, when the human population became concentrated in various locations. Religion developed as individual leadership evolved with the heads, families or tribes. Later, monarchies started to affect people's beliefs, and people began to project their social concepts onto the subtle sphere of nature. Those concepts were then confirmed by religious leaders in China, India, Babylon, Greece and Palestine, with the resulting development of strong religious monarchies. This trend, which continued under Christianity, has profoundly affected western culture.

It is a great misfortune when people lose their connection with nature. In the West, intellectual development conflicts with spiritual interest. This restricts scientists to the material sphere and excludes spiritual reality. In the social sphere, political leaders do not know how to set a natural direction that serves the well being of all lives.

Tao is not a religion. This very old, yet very new, direction unites all three spheres of life — body, mind and spirit — and could be called the Integral Way that encompasses the natural vitality of all lives.

Although spirit is the central aspect of life, it is neglected by the modern mind. It is my wish, through this and all of my books, to bring together the ancient and the modern, East and West, the intellectual and the spiritual in order to improve the lives of everyone I can reach and produce a united effort that will support the well being of each individual and the world.

III

Although each person experiences life and death, one thing is certain: there is universal vitality. If we harmonize with that universal vitality, we can live longer and enjoy life more, but we are usually so focused upon material goals that we forget the root of life: our natural vitality. That forgetfulness causes all our troubles.

What is called soul is actually the universal vitality of each individual. It is a kind of subtle energy that is not as solid and heavy as physical energy; it is more essential.

If a doctor treats a patient, how can the patient get well? A patient gets well mostly by his own natural vitality. Any healing method, herb or medication works by removing the external invader or the poison created in the body, thus stimulating the patient's own natural vitality to do a better job in restoring the health of a particular organ or part of the body that is affected. An old friend who practices homeopathy estimated that 95% of all disease was cured by the strength of the patient, and only 5% by the treatment.

Taoist medicine, which I also call integral medicine, differs from Western medicine in that we offer ways to prevent trouble from occurring in the first place by using natural energies in the form of herbal supplements, to keep a person at his maximum natural vitality. The focus of such a treatment is different from that of western medicine, which is concerned primarily with symptoms. We take an organic view of life, while modern medicine generally takes a mechanical view.

My understanding of natural vitality is that, in prescribing medicine, there is a range of 5% to 25% in which the medication is effective. In other words, a person who is sick uses 75% of his own healing strength to help himself; this natural vitality is the source of self-recovery. Even if a patient has a serious disease, his recovery still depends from 50% to 75% on his own strength. The healing power that comes from medicine is only 5% to 25%. If the vitality of a patient is low, then integral medicine works to build that vitality at the same time that it treats the problem.

A person with 100% vitality is a healthy person. When that person is sick, however, his healing energy is blocked or weakened and he needs external help from a doctor who must choose the correct treatment. Let's say that a healthy individual becomes 10% ill. Most western treatments are going to be too strong because they are determined by symptoms alone without taking the patient's vitality into consideration. If the patient is only 10% ill, a 30% cure would be too much and could actually harm the patient's natural vitality. Herbal medicine can be adjusted to the need and health of the individual patient. In fact, if the dosage is less, the recovery is greater, because it does not harm the natural healing power of the individual. Medicine should not cut down the young crops to keep the birds away, nor cut down the tree for the purpose of getting rid of the bugs.

In the use of natural healing modalities, only part of the treatment directly fights the disease; its primary purpose is to help enhance the vital force to fight the disease by itself. The body has its own wisdom of how to heal itself, and most of the time, it does its job quite well.

This illustrates the important principle of *wu wei*, which means "do nothing extra." Something extra might interfere with the wisdom of the body. It is best not to fight a physical problem but to let the life force itself take care of things. Taoist medicine makes no excessive invasion on a patient's body that would become a heavy burden to the vital force.

For example, sometimes young children have a fever in reaction to a virus. Generally speaking, a parent can give the child some ginger or leek soup or some mint tea or a warm bath, and sometimes these simple remedies can disperse the virus through perspiration. These are natural cures for a young person; however, modern people would rather use antibiotic injections to decrease the fever. This is like sending an entire army against a single thief.

The best healing method is various *chi kung (chi gong)* practices that build the natural healing force of the patient. This approach involved no medication at all. Natural vitality involves all three levels of life: the body, mind and spirit. People may laugh and say, how can the mind be a source of natural vitality? What they do not know is that the mind is a form of natural energy; it takes energy to think. A person must not be confused by external appearances of the mind, such as behavior, conception or emotion; a person needs to see what is behind the mind. In two words, it is natural vitality.

On the level of natural energy, human beings have not brought anything into the world or created anything new. Anything that is unnatural is neither necessary nor helpful. For instance, if a young person has a car accident or a disease, and is in a seizure or coma, modern medicine can technically keep such a person "alive," but it cannot restore the conscious mind. This is because it has no consciousness of the deep level of vitality, which is the level of spirits.

Keeping a physical body alive is only a modern method of mummification. There is no soul there. It isn't even on the level of what the ancient Egyptians did, however, because perhaps the soul of a truly mummified corpse can reenter the body, but the life of a person who has become a vegetable after losing the soul cannot be considered to be life with complete natural vitality.

Natural vitality can express itself at different levels. The first level is the physical level of the body, which is the foundation of the second and third levels, which are the mind and spirit respectively. In this book, I cover mostly the first and second levels, with some attention to the third level.

I encourage people to learn about all three levels and to reevaluate the natural achievement of our ancestors, who were not as enthusiastic about creating religion as their descendants have been during the last 3,000 years. Rather, they worked on nourishing their natural vitality and on attaining and maintaining balance among the three spheres of energy in their lives, with the result that they

became models of well being and a natural healthy life.
On many occasions, people ask what I teach. My teaching presents the truth of life as a whole rather than one
part of life or another. I believe and hope that you will
benefit by reading this book about the vitality that is your
natural birthright.

Ni, Hua-Ching
November 8, 1989
Los Angeles, CA

Chapter 1

The Life Force Sustains Your Survival

New Year Celebration
Year of Serpent Energy

Dr. Daoshing Ni: As we gather to celebrate this new year, let us forget and let go of the old year that has passed.

We will begin with the dedication to our masters and grandmasters. (*Nine strikes of the gong.*)

As T'ai Chi divides,
    Heaven and Earth are spontaneously manifested.
Clear, light energy
    becomes the Heavenly Realms.
Dark, heavy energy
    becomes the Earthly Realms.
In a human being,
    the energies of Heaven and Earth unite.
We cultivate Tao
    in order to evolve
    and become spiritually everlasting.
The secret of Tao is transmitted to us
    through our divine teachers,
    and through studying the sacred books of Tao.
May the Heavenly Jade Emperor,
    the source of all Divine Immortals
    who resides in the Golden Shrine
    of the highest Pure Realm,
    please accept our dedications.

(Three salutations)

May all divine spiritual beings
    who evolved from the universal spiritual nature,
    including inspired sages and virtuous human leaders
    of different times and places,
    please accept our dedications.

(Three salutations)

May the powerful spiritual energy
  of wealth, health, peace, happiness and longevity,
  and the heavenly shiens who respond to our sincerity,
  and all divine guardians within and outside of this
  shrine please accept our dedications.

(Three salutations)

May the harmonizing spiritual energy
  of loving union please accept our dedications.

(One salutation)

The creative energy of Heaven
  is our paternal source.
The receptive energy of Earth
  is our maternal source.
All people are offspring
  of the same universal origin.
Within my own true nature
  are the same virtues
  that belong to the great sages.
My sincerity is as deep as theirs.
I recognize my spiritual practice
  with my spiritual family
  as an expression of divine order
  and harmony in my life.
I have love for all people
  who are in their "winter" years
  and wish them to live enjoyably.
I treat all young ones kindly
  and help them to have a good life.
The sick and needy are also
  my brothers and sisters,
  so I protect and shelter
  them under my wings.
I assist the talented
  and do not waste my own talents.

If I enjoy a good life
and have many things to give,
it is nature displaying
its benevolence through me.
If I have little and undergo many difficulties,
it is nature building me stronger.
Only by realizing my pristine nature
can I fulfill the true significance of life.
To ignore the true significance of life
is to sacrifice my spiritual integrity.
To violate the normalcy of my true personality
is to undermine my natural well-being.
By following the principles of change
and always doing my best,
I hope to be in harmony
with the enduring will of the universe.
I gratefully accept what life brings to me
and do not cling to sorrows
or try to run away
from the reality of my life.
With courage I follow Tao
and obey the subtle universal law.
Rather than lose myself
by seeking the luxuries of worldly life,
I cultivate positive spiritual energy
in order to actualize a good life.
I follow only what is good
and thus never stray from my true nature.
When I transform,
my energy returns to the infinite source of life.
There is never a question of my existence or non-existence,
because beingness and non-beingness
are both aspects of my true nature.
I confirm the benevolence of the universe
through my selfless service to all beings.
The benevolent universe
sustains me with eternal life.

Please recite together with me:

From the five directions
*   comes the positive energy*
*   that brings a hundred blessings.*
All diseases are eliminated
*   and ten thousand miseries vanish.*
The spirit of the three origins protects me,
*   and the eyes of 10,000 shiens watch over me.*
My life is peaceful and trouble free.
Because I unite my heart and mind with the eternal Tao,
*   the universal will and my will become one.*
Because your younger brothers and sisters,
*   sons and daughters follow the Tao*
*   and use this tradition as their vantage point,*
*   divine spiritual beings often visit our shrine.*
With a hundred salutations,
*   your humble disciple is bathed in divine energy forever.*
We pray your longevity will be boundless
*   and your spiritual effectiveness will continue eternally.*

(Three salutations)

Thank you.

Master Ni: Happy New Year, everybody. First I would like
to share my new year's message with you.

The purpose of my life is to increase the good life
*   of all people and all creatures.*
The mission of my life is to continue the life
*   of the universe.*
The direction of my life is:
*   first, to be the essence of all human life;*
*   second, to be the conscience of the world;*
*   third, to be the mind of universal nature;*
*   fourth, to continue the achievement*
*   of all ancient sages;*

*fifth, to be the point where future generations
can harmoniously meet each other.
For these reasons, I live and work,
and make all possible efforts
to remove any obstacles to my goal.*

This is my new year's message to all of you.

This year we finally developed a school of integral medicine known as Yo San University. This medicine was the legacy of my father to his descendants. I am grateful to Dao and Mao and many other friends for putting this school together and giving me the title of President.

The foundation of integral medicine and its principles are exactly the same as those of spiritual cultivation. This is why it is worthy to talk about it on this occasion.

Chinese medicine developed from an integral vision of nature. Each individual life is composed of many conditions. Once those conditions change, the life also changes. Some conditions cannot be changed, but others can be, especially internal ones like thoughts and emotions. If a person does not change those conditions, especially internally or within his own living environment, and he insists on saying, "This is just the way it is," then there is no help for him.

Each individual is like a small world with its own environment of body, mind and spirit. For example, an eel can sleep and live in water for months. If we put an eel in the desert, it cannot live for long. Have you seen or heard about yellow fire ants? They have tremendous vitality, but if they are ever put into water, their life energy is instantly extinguished. Thus life is a matter of harmony with your environment.

Each life is an expression of its environment. For example, some people like to drink alcohol, but drinking can cause the spleen and liver to become swollen and eventually harden. Drinking also weakens the heart by constantly exciting and sedating it. If such a person comes to a practitioner of Chinese medicine, the first thing we will say is, "Please stop your drinking." In a case like this, you have to change the condition before you can restore the person's health. This is one type of healing process. There are different approaches such as, "Go ahead and keep drinking if you want to. We can simply remove your spleen or liver and transplant your heart, and you'll be just fine!" They can do it, too!

If you live a hypertensive way of life and wish to amass material gain, this can weaken your heart, which will then harden. Natural medicine will advise you to cut out some activity or reduce your ambition. Once you change those conditions, you can be helped; we do not recommend treating the body like a car with parts that can be replaced. I am not against organ transplants, I am just saying that it is better to control and watch the conditions of your life before they become extreme.

Because we are affected by different kinds of conditions, we need to strengthen our spiritual energy and develop our capacity for discernment. This process is called self-cultivation. It not only benefits your health, but the correct functioning of your mind and the full development of your spirit as well.

So the basic principle of Chinese medicine and spiritual cultivation is integral beingness. It does not treat people like machines. Nor does it take the attitude that if you have a pain, I can simply cut the nerve so you don't feel it, or if you have a cold, I can give you a medication to suppress the symptoms.

Chinese pathology takes your natural environment and emotional condition into consideration. Modern pathology is not usually associated with psychology, but they are in fact realistically connected. For example, if you become angry too often, the tension causes a secretion; your internal organs work harder, and this produces a poisonous gas inside. These poisonous gases can pass into the organs and cause heart trouble. Women can develop breast cancer, circulation problems, and female organ problems without ever knowing what caused them, because people are never taught that emotional matters can affect their physical health. Your own life force is the best medicine you have. It is better than any discovery, past, present or future; it can kill any germ. Let us take the example of two people. One has good energy and a strong life force. When this person is exposed to germs, there is usually no problem. The other, whose vital energy is weaker, has a greater possibility of becoming sick or infected. I would like you to increase and protect your life force instead of worrying about getting sick from contact with other people. Sometimes you cannot avoid being in contact with many people because of your life activities. The most important thing is to cultivate and strengthen your life force.

A human being is so active and beautiful, but an individual life is a combination of small lives that form a company or corporation. How to manage and even change your partners is an important spiritual practice. You might only be intellectually curious about this, but you might also take me seriously. I can teach you to tear yourself apart, but not through an operation. By developing your spirit, you can see and examine the millions of small lives that make up the one life that is called you. You are the one who is responsible for each small life inside of you. When they are sick, you are sick, because your mind is not developed enough to say, "Do not bring any trouble into my body, my mind or my spirit."

Last summer I was on a small island in the Northwest where I could be by myself and walk among the trees, which is the thing I most enjoy. I saw that many trees had died. I kicked one and took off the bark to look at it. There were a lot of termites in it. In that same group of trees, many were still very much alive. Those trees secreted a kind of acid over their bark that made the ants and termites uninterested in eating them. Only the weak trees were attacked.

Do not allow any spiritual termites to grow within you. Strengthening your life force is the foundation of Chinese medicine and your own self-cultivation.

As students of Yo San University, there is one important thing to learn: to become developed or to be a Chinese medicinal practitioner, you need a power. Perhaps you think I mean magic or psychic power. They might be associated, but the greatest power is sincerity. Some people are geniuses or have special talents, and that is admirable. It is a natural gift that is not connected with personal achievement. Personal achievement requires the power of sincerity. If someone else takes one minute to do it, you might take one hour to do it. If people take one hour to learn it, you might take ten days to learn it. But with sincerity and perseverance, you will achieve yourself. All psychic or magic power, if it is true, comes from the sincerity and perseverance of your own spirit. If you do anything to bring success to yourself and to your life, but lack sincerity, nothing will happen. You will not be happy. If you ask me if I have any secret, I might say, "I'm good at wearing out my helpers. I write and do so much that I exhaust them." They are younger than I am, but maybe I am really the youngest. Why? How? It is the sincerity and perseverance of my spiritual energy. That is the secret I share with you today. I hope that all of you can bring success and joy into your lives.

Malibu, California
February 12, 1989

Chapter 2

The Universe is an Energy Egg

Let us examine how we form our opinions about the universe and how we conceptualize our lives and our position in the universe. It is an age old human desire to seek answers to such questions as, "Where do we come from? How did the universe begin?" This evening, I would like to share the theories or myths from this very old tradition. How the universe began is not just a matter of intellectual curiosity, but a practical and useful area of consideration. Discovering the answer to this question can help us to decide how to organize our lives, enable us to understand life and death, and provide solutions to spiritual problems and questions.

Based on their observations of nature and how eggs function, the ancient developed ones concluded that the universe began as an energy egg. To them, the universe was the egg that contained all unformed eggs and seeds. Of course, no one can prove a theory, but I think people have a right to make guesses about such matters.

These ancient sages continued to use their spiritual achievement and spiritual vision to further develop their understanding. They did not know how long it took the energy egg to evolve, but they said it was a long, long time and that it is still continuing to evolve.

At the time it began to evolve, the energy egg started undergoing internal changes such as alternating expansion and contraction, heat and cold, and variations in density, until gradually, the world was formed. The first life came from these internal movements within the egg and eventually took the shape of a large being called Pang Gu. The ancient achieved ones considered him the ancestor of all lives, although essentially Pang Gu is simply another name for the universe itself.

We can imagine that, just as the life within an egg matures and finds its way out of the shell, so Pang Gu became active and started to grow. Thus, the universe formed just like a young life growing slowly inside a thin membrane and began its life with a sudden stretch.

The ancients also believed that Pang Gu's head became Heaven or the sky, his body became Earth, and his spirit, combined with the other parts of his body, became the power that forms lives, including human life. So all lives, all beings, all things and all stars are part of the body of Pang Gu. All of it is one being.

Another way to look at it is to imagine the universe as a mother pig that has conceived twelve piglets. We are the piglets. You and I were in the energy egg. Then there came a time that we were mature enough to become independent outside of the egg, so then we stretched and popped out. This is the result of the process of self-creation. The universe and the contra-universe, life and contra-life are presented at the same time.

Some people say that a big bang happened. I did not hear it. Did you hear it? Because nobody was born before the universe existed, this big bang can only be considered a theory, not the entire truth or reality.

Each egg has its own life, and we are all small eggs in a big egg. But not everyone looks like an egg; some people are egg-headed and some are onion-headed. In peaceful times, onion-headed people rule, and in wartime, the egg-heads rule. Before any type of head developed, everyone continually made trouble. I believe that neither egg-headed nor onion-headed people can be totally helpful, unless they become the Heavenly-headed. Human life, remember, is a small model of Pang Gu. Heaven is his head, Earth is his body and the breath (also called Man) is his mind.

This whole theory of the energy egg that I have described has profound implications for our individual lives and how we understand and organize ourselves. If you are serious about improving yourself as a small life in the universe, you can make use of this vision through integral spiritual achievement. Not only are each of us like an egg-shaped energy nugget, but many smaller eggs, with various shapes and functions, compose our big egg. When a group of smaller eggs are integrated as one big egg, we have life. When the egg disintegrates, we die. Death can also be a stage of transformation to higher spiritual evolution for some individuals. Real life is not limited to the level of what is visible, audible and tangible. It also includes the subtle level, and this knowledge about eggs can help us understand the reality of our lives and their relationship with nature. Among our many faculties, the mind is usually the one that enables us to manage our body and our surroundings. Within our own physical nature, however, even the mind is a piece of shaped energy. Interplay, union and activation never stops among the different eggs. This is the reality of nature, yet it is not too profound to see. I hope that you will pay attention and begin to study it, because it can be useful to you in organizing your life.

The Taoist theory about how the universe started is different from theories that are derived from an intellectual mind without spiritual development. Some philosophies say that the world was started by an omnipotent creator. Others say the world is merely matter. When anyone insists that their view is absolute, confrontation is born and groups begin to fight each other.

To the ancient ones, there was no problem about whether the universe started by mind or matter. An energy egg cannot be defined as either mind or matter, because it is just energy. Energy is life. If the universe is not energy, it is a dead, empty shell. It could not be you and me; it could not be life.

The great sage Lao Tzu, when he was quite old, still thought he was in the womb of nature. He said, "I am still enjoying living in the egg. I also regard myself as an egg." His work, the *Tao Teh Ching*, expresses the virtue of spiritual completeness, like the energy egg of nature.

In today's world, people can do many things that are far more complicated than what our ancestors did, but objectively speaking, not all of these things are truly serviceable. I suggest that as living entities, we are no greater than the egg from which we came.

There is no question that there is great diversity among

the people of the world. In China, for instance, hundreds of different tribes exist. Though all of them have yellow skin, there is not a clue that they all came from the same source. Each group has a different myth about its origin as a tribe, and these myths all differ except for one detail: each tribe thinks its people are the only descendants of Heaven. None think themselves less, but each thinks itself more than the other tribes. Each of them thinks their tribe is the only one that has a divine origin and that the others are mutts.

The egg-shaped symbol of *T'ai Chi* represents the importance of coexistence. One side of the *T'ai Chi* symbol is black and one side is white. Another ancient symbol showed two human shapes, one male and the other female, with snake-like lower bodies that were intertwined together. This image originated from two prehistoric sages: a man called Fu Shi and a woman called Neu Wu. These two sages were quite influential in their time as well as in future generations. They were each leaders of separate tribes, but by recognizing each other's tribe as brothers and sisters, union occurred and mutual benefit resulted.

Five thousand years ago, there was a war between the Han people, led by the Yellow Emperor, and the Nine United Barbaric Tribes, led by Chih-Yu. This war symbolized the competition between the spiritual directions of each tribe. The victory that was won by the Yellow Emperor demonstrated and reinforced the principle of coexistence, because, following his victory, he did not punish the defeated tribe but invited them to join his kingdom. The need for coexistence is the spirit that the *T'ai Chi* symbol expresses.

I would like to tell you one more story from China's long history. I think that this tribe's example can be relevant to the way in which you organize your life. In Santung Province, close to the ocean, stands Tai Mountain. For thousands of years, it was the custom for the leader of the country to pay homage to Tai Mountain. The leaders of China were not just leaders, they were the symbolic center of the country. As part of their spiritual practice, they would travel to Tai Mountain to pay homage to the subtle universal law. They would then carve their names there, just like tourists do today. Around 2,500 years ago, people could still see the carvings that leaders of different generations made on the stones of Tai Mountain. Do you know why those early rulers were interested in traveling there to make those carvings? This is an important spiritual truth, and I think it is important for you to understand. They believed that any ruler on earth is temporary. After many generations have come and gone, only Tai Mountain is still there. So they considered Tai Mountain the true sovereign of the earth, and their pilgrimages and carvings symbolized giving their sovereignty back to Heaven.

A group of ancient scholars wished to find out the meaning of these carvings, because originally there were no written characters or letters, only pictures that represented a tribe or race, or perhaps a dynasty of one particular family. These scholars eventually gathered information about the people who were pictured in the carvings and determined that the human race is 2,760,000 years old. There was a lot they understood from the pictures and a lot they did not understand. Although the carvings no longer exist, we know one thing for sure: at that time, no country or society was a police nation. There were no policemen. Their social system was not established by force. There were fewer people and their lives were simple. If anyone served as the symbolic center of the society, it was because they had done something of great benefit for people that earned them respect and recognition as king (*Warng*) or Emperor (*Ti*).

In those days, the words "king" or "government" did not mean what they mean to us today. They were expressions of natural energy, such as the strong energy of the sun (日) or the stem (杂) that connects a leaf or a fruit to the tree. If your neighbor did some good thing and became prosperous, you respected him as a strong energy like a king. That did not give him the right to collect taxes from you; it was a different concept of leadership. At the time that kings were spiritual symbols of society, China was also unified spiritually. Later, that spiritual unification turned into the rigid political unification of an empire. Even so, that empire was not like the empires of Western European history.

When history began to be recorded, about 2,500 years ago, the great confusion of Chinese society began. Everyone wanted to organize a force to take control of the country, thus violence and competition began. This caused sages, spiritual leaders and intelligent people to respond by trying to correct the growing problem. There were three main schools that offered solutions to the problem. Each teacher took some part of the spiritual achievement from the past 2,760,000 years, including good ways of handling problems, and based their teaching on it. So the teaching that came to be called the Integral Way was really the combined achievement of 2,760,000 years of human experience. This body of knowledge is not merely a philosophical presentation, but rather an education in how to realize oneself in life. That is what we call Tao.

Tao is not the short life experience of one person. It is the total life experience of all human people. Today we go to school and learn what has been recorded in the short period of written language, but we must remember that before the development of writing there was a long history of human experience. Those early human experiences are the treasures of life which cannot be lost. The effective ways in which ancient spiritually achieved ones learned to tackle and solve problems are the spiritual principles of this tradition.

At that earlier time, when the confusion of society first began, three sages who tried to tell people about the long span of human experience were Lao Tzu, Mo Tzu and Confucius. Each of them described Tao differently.

Most of you have heard of Confucius. He said there were only two important elements to Tao, the way of all survival: love and justice, or in other words, kindness and righteousness. He said, "We cannot do anything against love or kindness, against justice or righteousness, if we wish to survive in this world." Confucius exerted great efforts to teach people to learn from their ancestors and not be confused by social turmoil and disturbance.

Mo Tzu also taught that the ancient wisdom was composed of two important things. "First," he said, "have unshakable faith in the impartial Heaven. It is not your Heaven or my Heaven, the Heaven of this race or that race. It is the single, impartial Heaven." The second thing that Mo Tzu promoted was universal love. "Universal love," he said, "is love for each person in the world. It is not practiced according to the closeness of relationships such as relatives, friends and countrymen, etc." He taught that universal love is everything. With universal love, justice can be extended. Without universal love, there is no justice. Kindness is righteousness, and righteousness is kindness.

Lao Tzu was much older than both Confucius and Mo Tzu. He was an historian, and he searched much further back in human history than the other two. At that time, Lao Tzu was the only person who understood the symbolism of the ancient pictures and who knew how to read the knotted ropes that recorded important events that happened before written language was developed.

Lao Tzu's main teaching was *wu wei*. This can be translated in two ways. Referring to society at large it can be interpreted as, "establish nothing beyond the nature of your life;" whereas in referring to an individual life it means, "do nothing against your own nature."

In achieving the wholeness of life, *wu wei* is different from the teaching of Confucius or Mo Tzu. Even if a person acts in a way that is righteous or kind, if the action is done against one's nature, the righteousness can turn sour, and the kindness can have negative results. Thus, one's spiritual nature will be separated. *Wu wei* is different, because by "doing nothing extra," one allows the two opposing forces to harmonize naturally in their own time. Mutual benefit is found at the point of balance between two extremes. However, your nature and my nature are one; they are both universal nature. Thus the cultivation of spiritual wholeness means to become the ultimate truth of nature. To achieve this, live with your spiritual nature and do nothing against it.

As a student of Tao, I would like to explain something more about Tao and *wu wei*. As an individual born into the world, what is it that you need to do to become a naturally completed person? What is the process of spiritual self-cultivation? From the knowledge that universal nature and individual nature are the same, being large and small energy eggs, it is possible to achieve internal spiritual self-sufficiency or spiritual independence. It is also possible to become self-contained. Let me explain this more deeply to you, because if I only lightly touch the surface, you will not understand and you will miss its value for your life.

In modern life, each person needs to be valued by other people. You work hard to earn respect or prove your worth to other people. You want to be able to say that you are "somebody" in the world. This psychological attitude brings a lot of trouble, pain and disharmony. It is different from the attitudes of the ancient sages and achieved individuals. They did not try to "be somebody," but enjoyed the fruit borne by their own tree of life and sought to fulfill what they naturally contained. Social status, financial security and luxury did not fulfill them. Their enjoyment came from a different level that was based on who and what they were. To be naturally content means to be what you are. This is the spiritual level of life.

But can we, in modern times, enjoy what is by nature self-contained? We cannot, because psychologically we are conditioned not to. People are struggling to prove their worth. They "need" to fight for recognition from other people. However, the true nature of life has not changed since ancient times, only our vision and our understanding of life have changed. In the last 2,500 years of human history,

I do not see any spiritual progress. Human insensitivity has increased, and people are looking for cheap external salvation rather than developing themselves spiritually. This problem has never happened before in the 2,760,000 years of prehistory. People now beg for help from imaginary religious or spiritual images and ignore the internal spiritual sufficiency that is each person's birthright. This inner source of love and help, that can be increased through personal spiritual cultivation, brings true spiritual independence and self-containment.

Humans have lost their connection with the earth, and because they feel disconnected from the earth, they feel lost and insecure. This spiritual and emotional insecurity drives them to look for a source of strength outside themselves to solve their problems.

Their ancestors said, "We have been on the earth for millions of years. We have struggled and have found our strength. Intellectually, spiritually and physically we can handle our own problems." They sought internal growth and internal strength to handle external problems, but their weakened descendants have erected false images to which they look for salvation like spiritual beggars.

People with inner spiritual strength are like rich people who can give help to others. I hope that some day everyone will stop acting like beggars and weaklings and recover their inherited strength.

Here in the United States, I have made many friends who have the same awareness of spiritual self-sufficiency that our ancestors had. The ability to be spiritually self-sufficient is the teaching I learned. I came to the United States to share it with you. I am a self-supported teacher; that is my tradition. I treat people as a Chinese traditional doctor, and I teach at the same time. The purpose of my teaching is not to establish a new religion, but to give you a new internal voice with which we can communicate with each other.

You might think I am idealistic about ancient people. Certainly their lives were poor, and their opportunities were

limited by comparison to modern standards. Yes, we are
certainly more technologically developed than they were,
but I would like to offer you some facts that might reflect
the actual progress we have made, or have not made, as
the case may be.

A wild elephant in its natural habitat can live to be 200
years old. However, an elephant in a zoo or a circus, no
matter how well provided for, only lives to around 80.
Again, a wild rabbit can live up to 15 years, but a domestic
rabbit only lives for 5 at most.

How does this relate to human life? Lao Tzu, who lived
in a natural environment, is said to have lived to be 250
years old. The average life span of a modern individual,
however, is 60 to 80 years.

We must admit that our lives are not natural any more.
When we have trouble, we do not know how to handle it
emotionally. Maybe we pray, but prayer is self-deceiving if
we do not let ourselves see the problem and the solution
clearly. Self-deception comes from the psychological habit
of being dependent. Rather, let us see our problems clearly
and respond to them naturally.

In my books, there are many discussions concerning
different aspects of life. I hope you can examine them and
gather some helpful things from this long-lived teaching
that can help you.

Now, if some of you have questions, please ask them.

Q: Do you believe that Jesus Christ rose from the dead?

Master Ni: What Jesus did is not a question I should answer. I try to awaken your spiritual nature. Then you can
answer a question like that for yourself.

However, the matter of whether a person can rise from
the dead can be answered by reading the biographies of
many early achieved ones who, after dying, left their empty
coffins behind. Later, people who knew them would meet
them in different places. Their new bodies were temporal
convergences of energy that would appear and disappear.

Many such experiences have been recorded and can still be read in works such as the *Taoist Canon*. I do not think any one religion or individual has a patent on such a reality.

Q: Do you believe that God created the world and humankind?

Master Ni: Your concern is "who" created the world. My concern is the content of the world and the quality of the creation.

Q: The Buddhists believe that if you pay attention to something outside yourself, you cannot achieve universal peace and oneness. Can you say more about Taoism and Buddhism regarding universal oneness and the original no-beginning and no-end?

Master Ni: Before I answer you, I would like to mention that in the long span of human history, when people's lives were not burdened by any unnatural conditions, no one worried about doomsday, because they knew that life is always changing. It is like the alternation between day and night and the changes of the four seasons. Sometimes life flourishes, and sometimes it withdraws from the surface of the earth, but it always returns. These observations were written into a book of symbols and words called the *I Ching.*

Buddhism is a religion that developed in relationship to the existing culture. Sakyamuni was born around 2,600 years ago and he never wrote a book that said, "You must follow exactly what I say." In the vast body of written material about Buddhism, we do not know if Sakyamuni talked or if it was the later sages and enlightened followers who produced the books and teachings.

Quan Yin, a feminine image of Buddha, provides encouragement for individuals to nurture their pure, kind spiritual energy. Maitreya, the Happy Buddha with a big belly and a broad smile represents acceptance and tolerance and the satisfaction of unfulfilled desires. Both of these figures are Chinese in origin.

Buddhism, however, has a different goal than Taoism. Buddhism uses the form of external religion to teach your mind, while the teaching of Tao is concerned with reconnecting your physical and mental being with your spiritual nature. There is a level of the teaching of Tao called folk Taoism, but that is very different from my tradition which goes back before written history, when people were still natural.

The real contribution of the teaching of Tao is proving the ultimate truth of nature. Through spiritual practices, an individual can prove for oneself the existence of the egg-like spirits or ghosts of one's ancestors that compose the human body, including the different spirits called *hun* and *po* which compose a human being. One can also experience the *chi* that circulates and penetrates the eggs.

The difference between egg-like spirits and the *hun* and *po* spirits is that *hun* and *po* are an individual person's spirits, whereas the egg-like spirits are a combination of different spirits.

I would like all of you to learn the truth by proving it for yourselves. I wish that a scientific authority would learn this secret, so that this knowledge could be of much greater benefit to the world. Such a person or institution could bring breakthroughs in modern science and medicine, improve culture and religion, and eliminate much confusion and contention in the world. The foundation of modern science is based on physiology, anatomy and biochemistry, yet there is still a higher, more subtle sphere. Through a special process, you can achieve that level and prove what I say.

Q: The fellow who introduced you mentioned that you teach internal alchemy. What is that?

Master Ni: Achieved ones believe that because a person is a *T'ai Chi* or an energy egg, certain internal changes can transform that energy to become like a newly created being. This involves internal generating, internal adjustment and internal harmony. There are practices for refining and attaining this internal situation. Internal alchemy is a process of sublimating different internal energies and is connected with the achievement of immortality.

Some people are still interested in the truth of immortality, even though they have never seen it. If a person pursues the science of immortality, he will find that human life is internally like a laboratory where different elements can be combined. From my training, I can give you the formula for immortal life; however, it is up to you to put it into practice. Even though you have the formula, it will not do you any good unless you work at finding the ingredients and putting them together. You can prove for yourself that life is not as shallow or as short as this physical reality that we see. Instructions for internal alchemy are found in many of my books.

True spiritual development does not come from satisfying one's intellectual curiosity, although we can use our intellectual training as a foundation for developing ourselves spiritually. We need a scientific attitude, but so far, I have not found another way to teach the ancient scientific method other than the ancient way of one individual passing it to another.

If a spiritual teacher charges you too little and you understand or learn the subtle information, maybe you will throw it away before you actually benefit from it, because you think it has no value. Then you will say the teaching is of no use. If a spiritual teacher charges too much, you will say, "Wow! It costs so much?" and you will not bother to learn it. Then again, the great knowledge of the teacher is of no use to you or the world.

You cannot put material value on spiritual teaching because spiritual truth is everywhere, and the correct understanding of spiritual truth is so valuable that it is priceless. Without correct understanding, however, the spiritual truth is valueless and useless, and can even be harmful to people.

Therefore, at this stage, I am working on preparing people, because as you understand more, you will learn the value of the spiritual truth.

I hope someday to teach a few people who have some true attainment in spiritual learning and then publish the results. It is my wish that the next generation will understand this important spiritual knowledge. Then no one will misguide anyone else any more.

So how can you help yourself? Self-study may not be enough for some of you. That is why we have study groups. The purpose of my talk here is to help you open new spiritual frontiers by studying the wisdom of millions of years of natural spiritual development.

As you begin to learn spiritual truth, be objective and do not put a limit on yourself by calling yourself a Taoist or anything else. Labels tend to place walls and ceilings around one's potential growth, and make you forget that you can always grow more. That is the fun of spiritual learning; it is a continuous opportunity for growth.

Q: What is the actual goal of spiritual learning and internal alchemy?

Master Ni: All of us, before we were born, were natural spirits. Once we are born into the world, our original nature becomes blurred by cultural and religious influences of the time and place we live in, which causes us to view things differently. By becoming attached to a limited view, rather than seeing the expansive natural truth, we create conflict. As people become more developed, they do not fight any more. They enjoy a different way of life that harmonizes with nature.

No one can say that he or she does not have any troubles. No one can say the world does not have trouble. What is the source of all this trouble? The source of the trouble is that each individual human being, and the world itself, is spiritually blocked by artificial points of view. Spiritual undevelopment is like a person who is young and short and cannot see what is on the other side of a wall. He has to wait until he grows taller to be able to see over the wall, even though people tell him, "I have seen what is on the other side of the wall, so listen to me. I will tell you how to grow straight and tall so that you can see too. I have written a book to make it easier for you to understand."

There are many books, truthful and untruthful, superficial and profound, but they are not better than helping yourself and seeing by yourself. The path of spiritual development not only helps you grow tall so that you can see what is on the other side of the wall for yourself; it helps you break down the wall. My teaching efforts are meant to help all people with their own spiritual development.

Q: Master Ni, what sort of practices do you do to keep yourself so lively and youthful?

Master Ni: I hook up with the golden egg, which is the sun; the silver egg which is the moon; and the smaller eggs called stars. The whole egg is called Tao.

You see, students of Tao think that the universe is a centered energy field. Once you find the source, you can hook yourself up to it. At least you know enough to not cut yourself off from it and lose the connection to your source of energy. Youthfulness, you see, is not a matter of age; it is a matter of what you hook up with. Many people do not hook up with the energy source, they hook up to their own emotional problems instead. Then instead of becoming energized, they become drained by their self-created obstacles to the universal light. The spiritual practice is to deal with only as much trouble as necessary, and to hook up with the universal energy source regularly.

Q: Master Ni, I have a hard time understanding these ancient developed ones that you talk about. I saw a movie about ancient people called "Quest for Fire," and they did not seem very developed to me. It is hard to imagine that everyone who lived 2,500 years ago was spiritually developed, although I can believe they were more natural because there were fewer people and they had more space to be alone.

Master Ni: You're right, not all ancient people were spiritually developed. In fact, the majority of people were not developed at all. Yet, the ancient developed ones did exist, and society benefitted from their existence. It was only around 2,500 years ago that history began to record them because the rising social turbulence made them more noticeable.

Q: Was there a particular event that led to the rise of confusion? Your description sounds like everything was peaceful up until that time.

Master Ni: Things are never entirely peaceful in human life. There are always misunderstandings and such. The difference at this time was the scale on which it happened. Before 2,500 years ago, conflict only happened on an individual and family level, but then, with the development of society into small kingdoms, the scale of competition grew as the kingdoms began to battle against one another. That was a new and unfortunate development that led to mass confusion. So the sages tried to do something about it.

Q: It seems to me, after reflecting on this question, that at any given time in human history, only a small percentage of people are spiritually developed, and they are usually the ones who work to educate themselves. But of course not all people with a higher education are spiritual.

Master Ni: That is partly true. Spiritual development does not have anything to do with social class, at least in modern times. In ancient times, spiritually developed people were the natural leaders of society because their achievements were respected and they were looked up to.

In modern times, however, spiritual development and learning are different. Anyone can be spiritually achieved, regardless of their position in life or their social status. The thing that determines spiritual achievement is one's desire for it. Someone can be highly achieved spiritually and not necessarily be a leader or in the upper class, although usually they do not do rough or negative work. Intellectual learning does not imply spiritual development.

Q: In your books you talk about many practices for developing ourselves. If you had to choose the most essential one for people who live the active kind of lives that most of us live today, which one would you recommend?

Master Ni: I would like to say something about your personal growth: one bite can never nourish you for a whole lifetime. You need to eat every day. Spiritual practice, whatever form you choose, must be regular, then you will grow. At different stages of your growth, you will learn more. Right now you do not understand or know the value of advanced practices. If you tried them and lost interest, then you would not benefit from them. This is why I encourage you to study and continue growing, so you can go far enough to get the big benefit!

Q: Master Ni, once someone is introduced to the spiritual path, they are sometimes drawn off. They may go back on and then back off again. It seems that they should know better, but is it an additional burden to those at a certain level of spiritual evolution to go off the path and then try to go back? What is the consequence of going off the path?

Master Ni: It does not matter. In the process of spiritual growth, you always go back and forth until you finally attain maturity.

Q: Is it harder for some people who are at different spiritual levels?

Master Ni: Internally and externally, a person always comes

up against his own personal obstacles. This is how you find out about them. When you start to make spiritual progress, you meet your spiritual obstacles. You notice them internally by certain thoughts that repeat themselves, or externally by difficulties or habits that throw you back onto the old way. Seeing the obstacles and going on and off the path is not a problem. Some people bounce around over a particular issue for years until they learn how to resolve it. When they resolve it, then their progress is great.

It is a problem when people think their obstacles are stronger than they are, which is not the truth. This is why we read the books first to improve our understanding rather than suddenly starting to do the practices. Once we attain sufficient understanding, then there is no worry about whatever happens in our learning and growth. In the process of natural spiritual assimilation, we read to gain understanding at the same time we work on ourselves internally and externally and do the practices.

Understanding is a power. Once you understand, then there is no more separation. In contrast with that, if you have a problem, you try to separate yourself from it. But once you understand the nature of a problem, then there is no more separation from it and neither is there any connection with it. If we do not understand a possible problem, it is because we have obstacles that have been created by our own negligence. Trying to push our problems or obstacles away does not lead to growth. The power of understanding is what transforms people's lives. No negligence can be overlooked.

Q: How can someone find God?

Master Ni: How can you find yourself? If you do not find your spiritual self, you cannot find God. First you need to develop yourself spiritually. Different tools can be used to see different things. For example, if you are looking for small germs or bacteria, you need a microscope, but to see the spiritual truth you need your own refined mentality

and your own virtuous life. On one level, finding God is
the cultivation of self-identity. People who are achieved
are God and are therefore able to know God. It takes one
to know one.

Why is there so much confusion in today's world? When
a person achieves himself as God or Tao, he is no longer
confused. How great it would be if everyone did that; what
a world we would have! Many political and economic
problems could be solved so easily if people were able to
see and achieve the spiritual truth. Seeing the truth is
achieving Tao.

God is personified Tao. Tao is unpersonified God. It is
an individual achievement, not the achievement of a society.
In ancient times, people had the attitude that if each
individual could achieve himself, then he or she had fulfilled
the goal of a good life and made a contribution to the
world. Such people often chose to stay in rural places rather
than pursue frivolous social activities.

When I was a young student, I saw that individual growth
was not equal to the growth of the totality. We need the
growth of the totality in addition to individual growth, but
the growth of the totality begins with individual growth.

If you go out into the street, do you feel relaxed? You
do not, because there are people out there who do not
know the truth of life. If they did, then the world would be
a safer place in which to live. Changing this situation is
important.

I put a lot of hard work and energy into helping people
learn the spiritual truth for themselves. I hope to make
individual growth and achievement a reality for all people.
If this happens, true peace and the real kingdom of Heaven
will exist everywhere in the world. Otherwise, it is only
words in books and is of no use, except to already awakened individuals. However, I would not want it to become
the source of more prejudice and fighting by people who
are still in the dark. What good is that?

This is why we need to deeply reflect on the spiritual
problems of the past 2,500 years. Some people look back

on the early ancestors and call them foolish rather than developed, which they truly were. They did not have the spiritual problems that we now have. Maybe, despite appearances to the contrary, we are progressing.

You are sitting here today because you enjoy the spiritual energy that is generated in this kind of meeting and from reading the books made from these lectures. Otherwise, why would you come here? You may have come to listen to the words, but what is more truthful and deeper is that you have come to experience a different kind of energy. Your spirit inspired you to come here, whether it appears that way or not. Can you understand and communicate with your own spirit? It takes a little time, but it can be done. Sometimes we do many stupid things against our spirit. Our spirit may know something that our mind does not know, but we foolishly go ahead to do many things against ourselves. Seeing our mistakes in these instances can be a catalyst for further understanding and growth. Since doing some of those things can harm us if we are not careful, I recommend that you not do anything against your own spiritual nature.

Q: In that respect, can you tell us something about taking other life forms for our own nourishment? I mean killing animals for food.

Master Ni: You are asking whether it is moral to eat meat or not, because eating meat involves killing an animal. My answer is that eating meat is a personal choice involving many factors. One factor is an individual's health and profession: some people need to eat meat to support strenuous physical work or if they are older. Some people need to avoid eating meat because they do mental work or do not get enough exercise. It is a personal matter.

When you eat the meat of an animal, then part of the animal becomes part of you. This is also true with regards to a relationship with somebody. For example, if you make friends with good, trustworthy people or the opposite kind of people, they affect you. Whatever you do or touch affects you. It is the same with eating: always choose healthy, clean food.

Q: Does Taoism consider reincarnation to be true?

Master Ni: Reincarnation is a natural phenomenon. Some religions base their teachings on the natural cycle of life, while others ignore it altogether. The general concept of reincarnation is limited to the idea of a soul entering a new physical life. This is one kind of reincarnation that is a natural process of self-selection. However, there is another kind of reincarnation that is ongoing. People who learn Tao recognize that the next part of their lives, with each decade, and even with each moment, is a new reincarnation. We reincarnate right now in this moment with refreshed understanding and spirit; thus spiritually we are reborn from one moment to the next. We can consider this fact as a general background to life.[1]

Q: Can you say a few words about how the I Ching was developed and how it can be most effectively used?

Master Ni: I have already given most of the details in my book, *The Book of Changes and the Unchanging Truth.* Very simply, the *I Ching* illustrates the development of the energy egg that I mentioned earlier. The egg is not always the same, but can change to become silly birds like us.

The first book to describe human development was not the *Tao Teh Ching,* nor the writings of Confucius or Mo Tzu. It was the *I Ching,* which describes the energies of *yin* and *yang,* the two forces that assist and oppose

---

[1]For more discussion on reincarnation, you may be interested in reading Master Ni's book, *The Taoist Inner View of the Universe and the Immortal Realm.*

each other. The ancient developed ones who composed the book had discovered the alternation between these two forces: first, good times come with good leaders and good energy; then the good energy relaxes, which allows the other kind of forces to grow, and bad times come. This perpetual cycle taught our ancestors wisdom and enabled them to adjust to the long down cycle of human growth.

This interplay between the two forces of *yin* and *yang* is what I refer to as the subtle law. This law can also be applied to the understanding of individual lives. Sometimes we can apply our energy correctly to attain a goal, and sometimes we cannot. Because one cannot always find the right solution, the right position or the right spot in which to apply one's energy, the *I Ching* is available to help one see more clearly. The sixty-four hexagrams represent different situations and can help you understand what you need to do.

Individual problem solving is only one way the *I Ching* can be used. The *I Ching* also describes all phenomena at the spiritual, physical and mental levels. Any level or aspect of life can be helped by utilizing this symbolic system.

What is the reality behind it? People of Tao say that there is subtle energy above us. It comes from the source. What is the source? What is the subtle energy? If I give you the answer, it is only my answer. You need to cultivate yourself to discover it for yourself. Then it will become part of your own personal power. All questions about subtle energy, spiritual energy or personal power can only be answered by each individual for himself.

Q: What cultivation can we do to help focus our own internal healing abilities so that we can heal ourselves and heal others as well?

Master Ni: This is a good question. First you need to live a quiet life so that you can see yourself and observe any disharmonies within you. Any problem is an internal disharmony, mentally, emotionally or spiritually. If you can quiet down and discover the disharmony, then you are above the disharmony and can find a way to heal it or resolve it. This tradition has all kinds of practices to assist your emotional, physical and spiritual health. This is the foundation that a person needs before he or she goes looking for higher achievement. I suggest that you read and study my books. There you will find practices that are related to particular disharmonies and how to solve them. That will prepare you to take the next step.

Q: Master Ni, are there any Taoist affirmations that would help us get through our western way of life and the anxieties we experience in everyday living?

Master Ni: We call them invocations, and they are contained in several of my books. *The Workbook for Spiritual Development* probably has the broadest selection.

Q: There are a lot of groups in the United States concerned with transformation. Are you familiar with any of these and what do you think of them?

Master Ni: You are talking about the level of psychological change. That kind of transformation is important and helpful for many people, and I always encourage people to improve their lives in whatever way is meaningful for them. However, spiritual learning goes still deeper. In our tradition, transformation refers to a person's spiritual power to physically transform themselves.

Q: What is the difference between most methods of meditation and Taoist meditation?

Master Ni: There are many kinds of meditation that are positive and helpful. Their primary goal is to help people maintain good mental health.

In general, we generate internal energy. Basically, there are two types of meditation. The sedating type suppresses your energy in order to achieve a peaceful state. The other type generates energy. Dynamic meditation does not devitalize people, it revitalizes them.

Q: In the past, the achieved ones have kept many of their practices very secret.

Master Ni: Yes, and they still do, but the primary practices are not secret. They are proof by and of one's spiritual attainment. With such proof, a person sees the fruit of his cultivation. Otherwise, one would start over again. Secret can also mean effective. My straight teaching contains the secret teachings of all ancient religions

Q: Every once in a while, some of the secrets come to the surface. Do you believe that too much information is not beneficial, or do you believe that the information is what it is and that's it?

Master Ni: I take responsibility for what I do and teach. I do not take responsibility for the teaching of others.

The secrets you are referring to are not on the level of language. If you are achieved enough, you know who knows the secret. If a teacher says, I am coming to teach you a secret, he probably does not know any secrets at all.

Q: What is the best way to start simplifying one's life?

Master Ni: Simplify your personal relationships first. Get rid of the nuisances in your life, and get rid of possible trouble from personal favoritism. Be objective and practical; see what is beneficial to you and what is not. Do not let anything pull you down or away from your goals. If you do something that pulls you down or distracts you from your goals, you need to correct it.

On the other hand, you need to value the things and the people that help your growth. However, most things are two-sided: they are helpful, but they also hinder you somewhat. Some things you feel good about and some things you feel bad about. You need to learn to evaluate what is ultimately helpful.

Now, we must conclude this discussion. I have told you about the metaphor of the energy egg, because the truth is not external like holding an egg in your hand. The truth is internal. My message to you tonight is to hold yourself together in one piece for further spiritual development. To do that, you must gather yourself first, then we can talk about more advanced spiritual development.

We have had a good meeting tonight. I have really enjoyed being here with all of you. Some day, I may come back to see you again, if my schedule allows. Public speaking is usually not a deep way of learning. However, it is a way for me to get to know you and for you to get to know me. Thank you.

Miami, February 16, 1989

The Hun Tun Meditation

When you are in meditation, be sure that you are in a state of perfect concentration. Do not allow yourself to be in an excited or drowsy state of mind. Attune your mind to be peaceful, quiet and joyous, like a glass that contains good water. Not even one tiny spot of dust is stirring in the clarity of the water. Keep your breath steady, with gentleness and depth.

Now, close your eyes. Because you are in a room with dim light, after you close your eyes, you see nothing but darkness inside of you and outside of you. In this way, you are an energy egg within another energy egg. You are nurturing your own energy egg.

You have already taken care to be sure that there will not be any external disturbances such as phones ringing, etc. Pay attention and do not allow your mind to create any internal disturbance. With this state of quiet and gentle nurturing, your spiritual energy will grow by practicing the principle of *wu wei*, which means to force nothing. Just keep yourself in a natural situation. You will attain many spiritual capabilities if you practice this.

After you have practiced this natural meditation for a period of months or years, even with your eyes closed you will see the lighted room in which you are sitting. Still, do not push or force anything. After some time, you will see the lighted neighborhood at night; the walls of the room and of the house cannot stop you. After another period of time, you will see how the surroundings lighten up by your own mental focus. Nothing can obstruct your transpiercing vision. You can see things that have already passed and you can see things that have not happened yet. Because things of the past and the future are in a different stage of energy formation, they can be seen and known by your achievement. The length of time it takes for a person of general health to achieve all this varies.

To know is not everything in life; to be is the most important thing. Thus, the achieved ones even worked to shut off the valve of the knowledgeable inner spiritual being of oneself. As Lao Tzu says, know the bright but keep to the dark. In this way, he lived to 160 or 260 years old, according to the authoritative historian, Hsi Ma Chien (145 - 80 B.C.E.) of the Han Dynasty, who worked on the material that Lao Tzu had gathered.

He also said, know to be wise, but keep being dumb. This means to keep away from temptation in order to protect your life energy. Do not pursue the transient excitement of the external world. However, after you have achieved yourself, you still know everything. If you wish, you can guide yourself correctly in life.

In modern life, we have so many pursuits. If you follow spiritual principles, you first cut off the less important ones and simplify your ambitions in order to gather your life energy back to yourself. Your life energy keeps running away all the time, have you noticed?

This practice is one of the most important achievements of two million years of human life experience. It was taught and continued by the ancient Taoists as their fundamental practice. Now, you have received it. If it is your interest to balance the two aspects of internal and external in your life, you might like to study and read Lao Tzu's *Tao Teh Ching*. You will benefit from realizing it to whatever extent your stage of life allows and accepts. Your spiritual development is coming soon.

Chapter 3

Each Individual
Is a Complete Energy Field

There is a Chinese proverb that says, there are many straight trees, but there are few straight people. I appreciate everyone who has the openness and capacity to allow another person to speak honestly. As searchers for truth, if we are not straight, we waste a lot of time and energy in reaching our goal. So it is better to be straight and not take any detours.

I gave a talk in New York City once, and because I said something about communism, some people who were pro-communist got up and walked out. On another occasion, I was straight about something else, and someone else got up and walked out. It is not my intention to give you a walking exercise today, but to see if your minds are open and whether you can relate to the possibility of learning something new. Because my background and training are different from yours, I might have something that you will find interesting and helpful. So this afternoon, let's see how my learning can serve you and perhaps help you see the truth of life and the truth of the world. In that way, we will not waste this gathering or your time and energy.

In the tradition of Tao, we do not promote external worship or mind control. We understand that each person is an energy field, with his or her own unique arrangement. Not only are men and women different energy fields, but two women or two men will also differ from each other. There are no two energy fields exactly alike in the universe.

On summer nights, when we go outside and look at the star covered sky, we can see for ourselves that nature is an energy field. No matter how large or small the being, all is energy. The reality of life, matter and all momentary phenomena is that they are independent and yet also interdependent energy fields.

This may be a new concept to some of you if you were told that you are made from water and dirt. That is not completely untrue, but you are also a specific energy field.

We can take this one step further. In the game of chess, there are pawns, rooks, knights, bishops, kings and queens, but it is their arrangement that decides if someone is the winner or loser. In the game of life, it is the energy arrangement within an individual that determines whether life's circumstances are favorable or unfavorable, advantageous or fatal.

It is easy for any of us, after developing the capability of observation, to feel differences of energy in places and situations. This spiritual power comes from leading a quiet life, meditating and practicing quiet movement.

For instance, when you enter a person's house, you will notice a certain energy arrangement or quality. Similarly, when you go to the market or enter an office building, the matter of becoming a winner or loser totally depends on how you arrange the different energies that are present. Do you know how to effectively arrange your energy field to meet a new situation? If you have this type of knowledge, you will be cautious, because the arrangement of your energy field will determine the outcome of the situation.

After several months of quiet meditation, it is easy for an individual to distinguish the different energies of people, places and even schools of thought. The same is true of companies, nations, and even mountains, oceans and rivers. The differences are subtle, even if you are not consciously aware of them. The first step in spiritual cultivation, therefore, is to develop your sensitivity so that you know when you enter or contact a new energy field. First, know what kind of energy is presented. If you do not know, you will not know how to deploy your pawns, knights and bishops correctly.

The second important step in spiritual cultivation is similar to the first and involves spiritual sensitivity. Let us say you meet someone. You are young, and you wish the other person to be your friend. Are you certain, after you have sensed his energy, that you understand his energy arrangement? If you do not develop your spiritual sensitivity and your understanding, based on life experience and study, you will not know whether the person is truly compatible with you. Some people are totally incompatible with each other. If you misjudge someone's energy and spend a long time together, you may eventually find out or understand that the differences cannot be reconciled. If you understand this at the beginning, you can save yourself a lot of time and trouble.

My father's personal hobby was geomancy. He liked to observe the shape of land and figure out its suitability for a house, farm or tomb. Geomancy is an interesting thing to study. I have not gone as deeply into it as my father, but I know that a piece of land can have a spiritual effect on a person's life. It cannot actually make someone prosper, but at least it will not cause trouble. Other places are good for burying a deceased person so that the person's soul can enjoy peace. And still other places can affect you spiritually.

The Chinese look for a place to build a house that is out of the wind and has good water; that way energy can gather. Once I was assisted by a real estate agent in locating a house in a beautiful location. The agent took me to a house on the side of a creek, but the house was placed so that the creek came directly towards it before turning away and flowing off to the side. The strong water flow toward the house made you feel like you owned the beauty of nature. However, I also knew, from my knowledge of geomancy, that the creek was an energy arrow coming into the house, and that the owner of the house must die from it. So I asked the real estate agent why the house was for sale. She told me that the house was designed by the owner, but after he moved there, he got sick and died. The shape of a house and the shape of an energy field can affect people. This is why the Chinese would rather choose a peaceful place; it might not bring great financial support, but neither does it bring harm. It is hard for modern people to accept the idea that a living environment is an energy field, and that it affects their lives.

People are educated by public school systems now, but

what I teach is different than how to make a living or how many countries are in each continent. The most useful education is self-taught; it comes through daily meditation and developing yourself to know different energy fields, how to handle energy fields and how to handle yourself. That kind of education can save a person much pain and suffering.

Do you know what the truth of spiritual reality is? It is your own spirit, which is the center of one energy field. Let's discuss the correct energy arrangement of a human life. The high spirit of the individual is the center or boss, and the mind is like a minister or worker. When the mind is boss, it dominates a person's life with intellectual information, which is always incomplete. This is important to understand.

Once you realize that you are a small energy field within the big energy field of the universe, you have learned something important. The next thing to learn is that your energy field has a high spiritual essence, or what some people call God. That spiritual essence can be perceived once you develop some spiritual discernment. It is not apparent like a tree or a car, so without quieting down, you will not know its existence. This high spiritual center, which is the wisest part of your being, should be the boss or center of your life.

What is the center of your energy arrangement? What is the most significant point of your life? This is something that cannot be taught or even well described. To know it, you need to gently work on and develop yourself. The inward quest for God involves the same difficulties as the outward search for success; it changes. Tomorrow, what you decide is true may totally contradict what you believe today. If your goal is to attain the truth, how can you be so assertive today? How do you know that today's truth is final? Whether a teaching is right or wrong can only be known after you are spiritually developed. For example, when you are a teenager, you know exactly what is right or wrong for you, but what you think now is probably

very different. Why? Because you have grown. It is important to have the capacity and tolerance to continue to grow
rather than rush into deciding that something is true or
thinking that you are already perfect.

So what is this teaching? What is Tao? Tao is a path.
What is a path? It is allowing ourselves to continually
grow and develop. If there is a truth to the world and life,
it is that life continues to grow and develop. The whole
universe, and all lives, are in the process of continual
evolution. By this I mean spiritual evolution more than
physical evolution. For millions of years we have had two
legs, two arms and two hands, but how much subtle,
spiritual evolution has happened internally in your life since
childhood? You may allow spiritual evolution to happen,
or you may not. If you become attached to some doctrine
that someone has taught you, it may become an obstacle
to your growth.

You are affected by what you think and what you do,
and because of this you need to take responsibility for
your own spiritual evolution by improving the arrangement
of your energy field. For instance, when you are in
meditation, you can quietly see your own shortcomings.
This is not a matter of psychological self-pity or
disappointment, but rather a level of mental clarity in which
true guidance can be received from your own spiritual
center. Your spiritual center is your best source of non-
judgmental self-reflection and self-understanding.

Many of you understand the things of which I speak,
and by your openness and generosity we can harmoniously
and peacefully converse. Often, people do not allow others
to express certain spiritual matters, because the
backwardness of the human spirit still exists throughout
the world.

A person's presence or energy field is a nonverbal teaching, and I have come here to present my teaching to you.
The truth of universal nature is not mine or yours, it is
everybody's. Why can't people accept this? Because when
a tyrannical nature is deeply planted in childhood, due to

fear, it becomes the source of spiritual undevelopment. Because the teaching of Tao is not tyrannical, this meeting is not a solo performance; I would like it to be fruitful and helpful to your lives. Your questions are welcome.

Q: As a student of Taoism for only a short time, I am experiencing some resistance to certain practices. As I cultivate and refine my energy, there is a feeling of the energy dropping instead of rising and feeling more pure. How can a young person control one's energy?

Master Ni: I understand. When you rushed around, as all American boys do, you did not know yourself. Now you have become quieter. You are also more aware internally. When a person decides to make such a change, his or her first discovery is their own sexual energy. Any man or woman who is healthy will not notice their spiritual energy when they first begin to meditate, but their sexual energy. It takes time to refine sexual energy and transform it into wisdom. You must have patience.

Each individual has three energy fields. The lower field or *tan tien* is the sexual center or field of reproductive energy. The region in the middle of the chest is the mental energy field, and the region at the top of the head is the spiritual energy field or *tan tien*. Each field functions differently.

Some people have a stronger mind and some are physically stronger. Through cultivation, you can discover if part of your energy is imbalanced. When you discover this, you will ask yourself, "Is this sexual energy or is it emotional ambition?" Usually, if you are able to ask that question, you have already achieved yourself to a certain degree. The self-discovery of your problem is an achievement in itself. Usually, your energy needs to be adjusted and attuned to the condition of a well-arranged energy field.

If you are sixty years old and start to learn Tao, which is what most people do, you may discover that there is no more sexual energy. Then what do you do? You need to regenerate that part of your energy. If the well being of all three energy fields is lacking, there is something wrong and you need to correct the imbalance in your life being.

Q: If one were to encounter a hostile environment, in the work place or in a family situation, how can balance be achieved, knowing that the soft overcomes the hard, but without becoming too meek?

Master Ni: Basically, the answer can be found in your question, but your question can be answered on two levels. At one level, you need to be spiritually independent. On another level, you need to be socially adaptable, which does not necessarily mean sophisticated. Many people are able to use their social sophistication to tactfully manage an unfavorable or hostile environment so that trouble does not happen or is safely avoided.

I think your question is deeper than that, however. Perhaps you are connected with a group of people or are part of a family in which it is hard for you to say anything to justify yourself. Expressing your differences would stir them up and accomplish little.

This can become beneficial if you can objectively observe what part of the problem is due to the lack of growth of those people or your family and what part is due to your own lack of growth. The first step is to see the problem of all the participants clearly. The second step is to understand that it is not a question of hostility, but a lack of understanding or growth. You need to have sympathy with people rather than confront them. You need to communicate with them on a natural level and live among them without withdrawing to the conceptual level. Avoid becoming argumentative; that only strains the nervous system of both sides.

You have an opportunity to rearrange yourself. The other side may be disappointed when they discover that there is no enemy and their energy has been diffused. What you may not realize is that in the past, maybe you were the one that harmed them in the first place. Once you see the matter differently, they will notice something is different. Then there are two ways that they might respond. One is to attack you more vigorously. The other is to mildly say you are unfair. However, in either case, just by the subtle influence of your gentleness, a difficult situation will turn out better. It all depends on how you handle the energy field.

When you have attained some growth and can see a problem clearly, you are able to rise above competition. It is as though you take the viewpoint from the top of a mountain while the other person still has the limited view from a canyon. Now that you are in a better place, do you think you still need to be nervous about it?

Q: *Master Ni, I have not read any of your books. Could you please tell me where to start? Which one is considered the most essential?*

Master Ni: If you do not have a specific problem, and would like to know the truth of life, I recommend reading *The Gentle Path of Spiritual Progress* and *Spiritual Messages from a Buffalo Rider.* If you are more intellectual, you might like to start with *The Way of Integral Life.*

Q: *Is there any danger in practicing sitting or moving meditation in an environment such as a hospital or a mental health facility? I work with people who are sick or mentally ill, and I wonder if there is any danger of taking on a lot of negative energy from that environment?*

Master Ni: Your question has different answers on different levels. If you are a beginner, you need to gather good energy to support your life, your study and your development. What energy should you gather? Definitely not sick energy or death energy. You may work in a hospital because of your great heart that cannot let you walk away from sick people, but even so, you still need to learn methods of purifying contaminated energy. You can get more information from my books or from my friends here. Any environment where many deaths have occurred is not fit for meditation. Let me give you an example. Once I accompanied several students who had no high achievement, but they had a pure life. We were looking at houses for sale, and when we entered one house, one woman walked out, vomiting. Some stronger ones walked through the whole house, but everyone felt bad, so I asked the real estate person about the people who had lived there. She told us that the boyfriend of the owner of that house died recently after having been sick in the house for many years.

So your eye cannot see and your ear cannot hear, but if you are a healthy person, you can feel. If you cannot tell a place with good energy from one that is bad, maybe you are numb from staying somewhere too long and cannot notice the differences. For your own virtuous fulfillment, and perhaps because you need to make a spiritual breakthrough, you have chosen hard work to do. When you come home after work, you need to purify yourself.

Q: Master Ni, can we learn from other traditions in addition to yours?

Master Ni: Basically, before a spiritual student is really achieved, he or she can wander around. I make no comment on other teachers. What I can say is to ask yourself if you have achieved enough from one teaching to go to the stage where you do not need to worry about becoming confused. If you learn for emotional reasons, you may need many teachers, because the level of emotion is still external. If you learn for spiritual development, then you are the one who must do most of the work because spiritual learning is internal. The teachings you choose confirm the level you have reached through your own efforts.

Many religions have teachings that are spiritually confusing. As a teacher, I take responsibility for what I teach. In the teaching of Tao, anything connected with life is our subject. So sex is a spiritual subject. However, some people use the word Tao to promote sexual indulgence. They call it the Sex of Tao or the Tao of Sex, or whatever. Then new teachers and students read about it, and after becoming involved with those teachings, many mistakes happen in their lives. This is an example of spiritual confusion. I teach a healthy body, healthy mind and healthy spirit as the foundation of spiritual development.

Q: Are there actual spiritual entities that assist humankind?

Master Ni: As a student of Tao, I have learned many important secrets. On one level, certain practices make semi-spiritual, semi-physical spirits appear. If you develop sufficient spiritual sensitivity, you can feel their presence and you can know them. I describe this in my book, *Nurture Your Spirits.*

These ancient discoveries about life can help modern scientists answer questions raised by inadequate knowledge in areas such as physiology, anatomy and biochemistry. Spiritual knowledge is not antithetical to science, the two can actually work together. Although the high spiritual level is too subtle for uncultivated people to prove for themselves, half-physical, half-spiritual spirits can be known, and their existence can be proven through certain practices.

I am looking for good students who will cultivate themselves without needing to satisfy their intellectual curiosity. I will give them the secrets that have been passed down for thousands of years so that they can prove this semi-physical level of spirit for themselves. Once a person proves this level of spirits, proving the existence of the high level of spirits is also achievable. A person needs a certain level of development to know high beings. I would like this to become common knowledge for the next generation of the human race.

Q: Master Ni, I would like to know what role art and music play in Taoism.

Master Ni: They are both elements of a good life. If they are without any oral doctrine, art and music can be a good form of religion. If they harmonize with one's spiritual nature, they can be especially inspiring and help one's spirit conform to the simple essence of natural beauty. About 2,500 years ago, great confusion came to China. Before that, people lived harmoniously; however, society changed when people became competitive over social glory and rulers became self-indulgent. So some sages came forward to teach and explain the ancient experience that had been forgotten, and how it could solve the present problems. What they offered was the wisdom from 2,760,000 years of human experience. One teacher, Mo Tzu, even rejected music. He said that indulgence in music caused a person to become scattered, and that it was of no benefit to spiritual students. It is true that anything, if used indulgently, is bad. Another sage, Chuang Tzu, who was a follower of Lao Tzu, also said that music scatters your energy. However, he added that bad music violates your energy, while good music can harmonize your emotions. Music can be one of the best cures for emotional trouble.

The principle of Taoist music and art is harmony. When you listen to it, observe how the music can make you enlightened. Good art and good music can harmonize you internally and externally. If that is achieved, the music or art is close to Tao. The highest level of art is formless, and the highest music is soundless. They abide with the profound Tao.

Q: Master Ni, I understand the need for simplicity, yet everything seems to be getting more complex. Would you offer guidance on how to establish priorities?

Master Ni: I believe you have not given it enough time, and your learning is not firm or clear enough. To gain in strength and in good decision making, you need to examine what you really want out of life, which things are really important to you. You are an attractive woman. This will cause complications in your life if you do not follow your deepest principles.

Because your question is abstract, my answer is also abstract. That means, work on it. If you work on it, it will improve. If you are looking for practical help, maybe you can find some experienced people in a study group and benefit from their experience.

This is a superficial answer to your question, but we cannot really go any deeper into it in public.

Q: I have been taking classes for t'ai chi movement and Eight Treasures for about five months, and they have totally changed my energy. I wish you would talk about t'ai chi a little bit and the benefits of meditation.

Master Ni: There are two kinds of exercise. Jogging, tennis, going to the gym and other similar sports mostly build muscles, but do you ever wish your body and mind could meet each other? You are always looking for new friends, but do you ever make friends with your own body? You can also benefit from making friends with your inner being. People generally do not do this, because the eye is built for looking outside. In fact, all the sense organs are made to gather external information, and they eventually cause you to lose contact with your own life. *T'ai chi* movement, if *t'ai chi* is a movement, is a basic practice to help you find or reconnect with your own life. It is helpful because it is practical and not hard to learn. It also improves your health and helps break up emotional obstructions. By practicing it, you can learn what energy or *chi* is. Any movement that is too strong makes you unable to manage the subtlety, softness and delicacy of an energy field.

In general, people chant or count their breathing and so forth in meditation. This is usually the first level. It seems sedating because it makes your mind calm and you feel good; it is almost like a drug. If you continue to do it for many years, you become devitalized. Spiritual self-cultivation generates energy and makes you strong. Not only do you feel good, but you will feel revitalized. *T'ai chi* movement will slow down the natural aging process that comes from exposing yourself to external difficulties such as the urban environments. Self-cultivation is an art and a science that can make your life endlessly enjoyable.

Q: Would you comment on the direction of the family in this country?

Master Ni: Many people have asked this question. Because society is internally empty, people seek either endless recreation and excitement or a way to become sedated. This usually leads to drugs.

It takes many years to achieve spiritual enlightenment. Drugs, on the other hand, provide instant change, but their side effects are very bad. People know that drugs are not a good thing to do, but they still take them because there is no other replacement for the kind of feeling they wish to have. Drugs symbolize a human condition. Cigarettes, coffee and alcohol all serve the same purpose. If they do not excite you, they sedate you in order to make you feel good.

Most spiritual practices are like drugs that offer easy, immediate satisfaction. Healthy spiritual practice requires effort, and unlike drugs, there are no side effects or damage to the body, mind or spirit. It enables you to ascend, not descend. At our clinic in Los Angeles, many patients are former drug users. Our first task is to teach the patient the value of life. If a person is materially well off, but still feels empty inside, he or she can easily turn to drugs or alcohol. Some people feel pressure from their spouses, then they turn to drugs for relief. Other people, because they are disappointed in themselves, use drugs as an excuse to not achieve anything. Or rather, they make trouble in order to get attention from family members or friends. Others are influenced by friends. The young, because of their curiosity, find drugs irresistible.

Drugs are not a solution to anything. It is hard to correct your own problems and find the right solutions. You would do better to focus on spiritual achievement. Once your mind or spirit is damaged, it is even hard for divine beings to help. Fundamentally, people must save themselves. This answer may not be as direct as you hoped, but it is useful.

Q: Can anyone achieve spiritual completeness, or does high spiritual achievement depend on a person's destiny?

Master Ni: A person can change his own destiny. I mentioned earlier that each of us is an energy field. What we call fortune is merely a specific energy arrangement. Whether one's life is favorable or unfavorable, successful or unsuccessful, positive or negative is always subject to new influences and new energy arrangements. It is strongly influenced by new behavior. When you are awakened by your own spiritual growth and new self-awareness, you know what is unfavorable, so you move your pawns and knights to different positions on the chess board of life and change your fortune.

Failure or success is decided internally before it is ever expressed outwardly. If you wish to be a successful person, you need to change your internal arrangement. For example, let's say that you enjoy riding motorcycles. Sooner or later, a person who plays with motorcycles will hurt his leg or body. If you really know that, then you will give up motorcycle riding as a form of enjoyment. If you do that, I believe the direction of your fortune will change immediately to something more rewarding.

Many young people enjoy speed for its own sake. Let's say that you are calm and you have achieved enough maturity to know that speed can cause a problem. If you stop rushing, I believe your fortune will change. It is very simple and very practical.

Say you have a sister, and she always does better in school, in making friends and doing other things, and you are always jealous of her. If you change yourself internally, then you will radiate light and become an attractive person.

This is much better than sitting there, being jealous of your sister. Many situations are like this.

So, to answer your question, destiny does not determine your level of spiritual achievement. Your spiritual achievement decides your destiny.

Q: Master Ni, in studying herbology, I was impressed by the many different kinds of herbs. Some are for healing the body, others are tonics for developing chi in the body and still another category is used for spiritual development. Will you speak about the herbs that are for spiritual development and how they work?

Master Ni: Your question is quite specific, and I hope other people are also interested. Generally, most people understand that herb formulas work. Do you know why they work? Many people come to me with, for example, chronic back pain, an internal problem or cancer. How can acupuncture treat these problems? The secret is simple. We observe each body as an individual energy field. We use needles and put them in different points to rearrange the person's energy. Though the energy habitually comes back to the trouble again, we always change the direction. Some people need only one session, while others will need many sessions. Finally, we succeed in changing the energy field of the individual, who then becomes healthy. This is one important principle.

Different herbal formulas treat different problems. Even if two people have the same problem, due to personal differences, gender or physical conditions, the formula is usually different, because each herb has its own individual energy. Some herbs are combined energies. However, arranging them in a formula will change a person's energy. This is the main treatment in Chinese medicine.

You asked specifically about spiritual herbs that can help people achieve themselves. In the book *Suhn Nuhn Pung Shao Ching*, there is a description of which herbs can make your body feel light and enable you to live long.

Ginseng, hu shaw wu, fu ling, sen di wang and so forth are not new. They were already on the earth thousands of years ago, and they took the energy from the natural spot in which they grew. You might eat them, and see how long you live. Even if you take a lot of vitamins and tonics, they are limited, because you cannot deposit them inside yourself like a body bank account. On the other hand, herbs themselves are a life. Some herbs live for over a thousand years. If you use them, then you are a life being with the energy of the age of the herb and your own. For example, suppose you are forty years old and you use an herb that took a thousand years to grow; you carry that thousand year old natural energy.

Some people eat a bunch of vitamins: gulp, swallow, and down they go. The vitamins are made in a laboratory, but how much energy do they have compared to the natural essence of herbs? If you use vitamins that are made in one minute, I do not know how much benefit you have taken in, compared to the power of a natural herb.

To get back to your question, spiritual herbs do work. Their properties were discovered by people who sought the secret of longevity by observing nature. I hope you are lucky enough to find those thousand year old herbs. There have been some people who lived on earth for many generations and who were spiritually immortal. We call them *shiens* or spiritual beings.

Q: Master Ni, would you comment on the AIDS epidemic?

Master Ni: Let me begin by talking a little bit about sex. If a person has sex, it should be out of natural instinct, not out of mental desire. Many people do not have sex because their body needs the adjustment but out of mental desire, because they are motivated by television or because they are emotionally restless and need to do something to release nervous energy. In that way, they abuse themselves. If they keep doing that, they will end up not having any sexual energy at all.

Sexual energy is the source of vitality. Once your vitality is low, then sex is not beneficial; in fact, it is harmful. All kinds of diseases will happen, even death. In other words, when you overdo sex, you lower your immune system and invite problems.

In one of my books, *8,000 Years of Wisdom*, I have given a lot of information about sex, pregnancy, and diet. I wish you would refer to that book.

About AIDS, the world periodically suffers from epidemics. Again, I will repeat the true spiritual knowledge that is helpful in any situation: live a quiet life and be moderate in your activity.

If you are interested in that, I invite you to examine and study my books. This is a great time for all of you to rearrange your energy field and attain a new life.

Talk given at Mercer University, Atlanta
February 19, 1989

Practical Applications

The following spiritual practices can help an individual rearrange his or her energy field.

Align your body correctly when standing, sitting, moving and lying so there is a smooth energy flow. When you are standing, the vertebrae should be gently straightened, as though the top of the head were attached to an invisible string from the sky. When you are in other positions, keep a similar straightness of the spine. Only when you are asleep is this position changed. At that time, the energy flow is very low and it is suitable to lie on your side with your legs folded in toward the chest.

The body's natural energy follows the cycle of the sun. From midnight to noon the energy flows upward, and from noon to midnight it flows downward. The one who knows how to ride the sun's route will organize his life activities accordingly. He will be most active during the upward arc of the sun's path from 7 a.m. to 3 p.m., and use the downward arc to gradually cease all activities. Managing one's schedule in this way may be difficult for some modern people, but it is good for organizing different activities. It would be better to schedule the more exciting and strenuous activities before 3:00 p.m. and leave the less exciting and strenuous ones until after 3:00 p.m.

Tea and coffee both stimulate the brain. It is better to live without them, because they interfere with the natural energy flow of your life.

In general, people should go to bed before 10:00 p.m. and get up no later than 5:00 a.m.

For young people who attend night school, if they are supported by generally good living habits and do not damage their bodies with drugs or sexual indulgence, a normal life schedule can be restored after finishing school. Working, studying and having sex all at one time burns the candle at both ends and harms a person's health.

People who work at night would do better not to stay on such an unbeneficial schedule after they are 50 years old. However, there are still two types of people: day people and night people. Nevertheless, it is still not a good idea to violate the life energy flow by a sudden shift or a very irregular schedule.

In sexual life, the worst time to have sex is just after midnight. A famous immortal wrote: "It is a hundred times more harmful than usual when people make love at the hours of Tzu (1:00 - 2:00 a.m.) when the *yang* energy of the person is just starting to sprout."

One cause of cancer is to make love when one is enraged. It is also damaging to make love after one has exhausted oneself by other activities. When parents-to-be make love during a storm or in any unfit time or place, it can cause the conceived child to become violent or insane, and so forth.

In general, stay away from the energy of sickness or death unless it is necessary, if you are the doctor or the relative.

Do not stay in a place in which you do not feel comfortable.

When you decide to buy or rent a new residence, you need to go to the center of the living quarter and stand there for a few minutes with your eyes closed. Let your feeling tell you about the place, in addition to considering other important things such as the water, the direction in which the door faces, the location, and whether there is too much energy interference and intrusion.

Do not wear the hat or clothes of other people unless a careful cleansing process has been done. Still, do not wear the hat of others. It implies that you take on the person's fortune, which is usually worn out.

If a relationship is as close as marriage, energy disharmonies sometimes cannot be foreseen, such as when the other person's cycle changes. If a relationship is not entered with spiritual discernment, but rather from emotional or physical impulse, it will usually be unbeneficial. Many possible soul mate couples become overly sexual at some stage. If they allow that to happen, then the spiritual benefit decreases and the relationship will end when the sexual interest wanes.

There are many things to learn about the maintenance and enhancement of the energy field of individual life. If you develop yourself spiritually, all of these teachings will be confirmed through your own life.

Chapter 4

God is a Name For Universal Life Energy

The Yo San Principle

Many years ago in China, when I was a student in my father's acupuncture school, my father told me and all his other students that integral medicine is not an external discipline. It grew out of two million, seven hundred thousand years of human life growth and is based on internal recognition of the problems of life. In this way, it provides effective internal and external solutions. What this means is that integral medicine is a spiritual awareness of life, slowly attained throughout hundreds of thousands of years of real life experience. As internal awareness grows, solutions become self-evident.

So my father told us, "To learn integral medicine, you cannot simply take what has been written in books and study that. You must develop yourself spiritually before you can become a true healer." He repeated this many times, and I am repeating it to all of you. Reading books is only one step to true healing. Going to classes is only one step; you need your own spiritual cultivation and awareness so that you can link yourself with the accumulated experience of human development.

What constitutes a spiritual awareness of human life? My father told us something very easy to remember and very easy to apply: a healer first needs to affirm positive life energy by learning about the positive energy of the universe and his or her own positive energy. The universe is nature, and nature is mainly an expression of positive life energy. Each person is active and does things right, because of positive life energy. Occasionally, this positive life energy becomes blocked or obstructed. Someone who has developed a spiritual awareness and capability can help restore the normal flow of positive life energy. Basically, the development of integral healing is the result of the experience and understanding of spiritually developed men and women. It is the accumulation of their external discoveries and self-discoveries and the solutions they applied to different problems.

People lived in China for centuries without any means
of communication such as we have today. For a long time,
they had to survive physically, mentally and spiritually,
without external help. Even formal religion did not develop
until 3,000 years ago. The people who lived in that enclosed
environment became spiritually aware, however, by learning
to recognize and develop universal positive life energy.
That became, in a sense, their religion. They worshipped
the respect, protection and love of the nature-giving positive
life energy in themselves, thus what eventually came to be
called Taoism was never an external religion.

God is just a name for the universal positive life energy
in each of us. By manifesting that energy in our lives, we
bring out the beauty of life and also some great achievements. Without that energy, nothing can be accomplished
in the world.

There was a popular philosophy in China that divided
the universe into four stages: birth, growth, decline and
emptiness or death. These philosophers stopped at the stage
of emptiness, however, without realizing the subtle power
of regeneration that is always there. People who fail eventually succeed; people who are sick regain health. People
who are poor become rich; people who fall rise. That power
of regeneration is the powerful force that we call Tao. It is
positive life energy. When a person supports that energy,
that is called virtue or morality or holiness. If someone
does something that harms it, their actions are wrong and
can be called sinful.

Although war and other human disasters are created by
spiritually ignorant and immature leaders, the regenerative
energy always brings forth life again. Although spiritual
people tend to not become involved in politics, we approve
of any political, healing, social or educational system that
supports positive life energy. As future healers, set a simple
standard for yourself: do only those things that support the
growth of positive life energy in yourself and others. If
something is harmful, do not do it. There is no higher
discipline than this. Although it applies to any individual

and any society, it is not an external doctrine does not matter what anyone calls it; what matters is that we apply it.

The second principle my father taught us was kindness. Protecting and developing positive life energy is kind. Cruelty, violence or brutality is harmful to positive life energy. No evil violent force can last for long. No extreme can bring true progress. Only gentle, kind progress can bring true maturity.

So you need to be objective about what you are doing and being, about the company you keep, about the schools you go to, about the church you attend: do they support your life energy or do they feed your swollen emotions? This is important to consider.

My father always liked to compare Taoist or integral medicine to a pot of boiling water: you do not stop water from boiling by blowing on it, you have to take the pot off the fire or take away the fuel that makes the fire. This fundamentally describes the basic principle of all treatment. Once you discover the trouble, you treat the cause of it, not just the symptoms. Treating a toothache or a headache alone is not enough. You need to discover the source of the problem. Once the real problem is solved, the symptom will not come back again. Otherwise, a person needs to sit in the dental chair over and over again. That is not healing, it is punishment.

Talk given at the open house of Yo San School of Acupuncture on April 22, 1989.

The Life Force Comes From Within

Although Master Ni no longer works in the Union of Tao and Man clinic, this meeting was requested by the couple and arranged by his sons who continue Master Ni's healing work in Santa Monica. The beginning of the discussion was the patient's description of his situation, which was not recorded. The second section of this chapter consists of questions about the material, asked by a student who helped prepare the chapter.

Master Ni: Let us see how we can tackle this problem, because your problem is serious enough to force you to see the opposite side of reality. First, I would like to share with you my tradition's philosophy of life.

Nature endows each of us with an abundance of life force so that we can accomplish whatever we need to do. Now, you have accomplished a lot in your life. I think nature has treated you well, for the most part. However, you might need to examine your attitude toward your illness. Is it something that you can possibly handle using your own life energy, or do you regard it as someone else's problem? You need to decide. For example, if I was in the entertainment business and I had a problem, I would come to you for advice. Similarly, when you become ill, you think like a customer who wants to find someone else to take care of your health.

Many people reach the limits of modern medicine and are on the verge of death before they finally turn their lives around and restore their health by their will to live, by new ways of living, and by forming new psychological attitudes and positive emotions. I do not need to quote all the stories. I know it is possible, and you know it is possible. Miracles happen to a miracle doer. It is not too late.

This is the main fight of your life. You cannot totally entrust your life to anyone else. Some things we can let other people take care of, but some things we cannot let other people do for us. For example, several years ago, you had some minor health problems. Even then we talked about your stepping back from your work and possibly beginning retirement. Those small signs were telling you something, but you did not like the idea, so your body slowly stopped cooperating with you. You are very good at what you do, and for you work is fun, but a person cannot always continue to do and be the same.

Now you must take one step back. This is serious, and it is telling you that you need to give up your work. How old are you?

Husband: Almost seventy-three.

Master Ni: When you work, your life energy goes into the work, but you need to withdraw that life energy from external pursuits and use it to take care of yourself. You don't think that way, because your philosophy of life has been different, but you can bring that energy inward.

Do not think "I need to get well fast so I can get back to work." Whatever happens to you, now is the time to reflect on things. When your old clients come back and ask you to take care of their problems, tell them "No, I need to take care of my own problem." Cutting off the burden of your business is a step toward psychological health. Mentally, it is time to gather your life energy back to yourself; taking care of yourself must become your first priority. Can you accept that?

Husband: I think I have pretty well accepted it now.

Master Ni: The second thing is, chemotherapy means your land has been invaded by an enemy and a doctor will send soldiers inside you to fight it. But while the army is fighting the enemy, the poison of the medicine will not only destroy the cancer, it will also destroy your crops. You see, my friend, at our age, we have only so much energy to sustain ourselves. Once that army is sent into you, it destroys your life energy too, along with the enemy.

Because you are still strong, there is an alternative. This is just a suggestion. When something like this happens to someone in my tradition, rather than taking chemotherapy, they will fast, because what you eat not only supports you but also supports the cancer inside of you. So what you might do is stop eating all solid food and begin fasting. By drinking only carrot or watermelon juice, etc., to sustain your life and your main needs, and by keeping quiet, an opportunity will be provided for the natural healing energy of your body to help you. A miracle might happen, if you stop eating regular food and expel the poison by yourself. Each person has natural energy in his body that fights such problems.

Any internal or external trouble is a warning to tell a person what should be changed. It is as if the body is a boat. A person sits in a boat, and if the boat is sinking, he must face it and abandon the boat, because spiritually he can still, with no harm, live in a different sphere. We will talk about that later. For now, we must talk about the best way to tackle the problem.

Husband: The conventional diagnosis of my situation was that the surgery that removed about 5 or 6 inches of the colon also removed the source of the cancer. But the leakage from the original cancer has now spread extensively in the five weeks since the operation. My doctor says that this is a life-threatening situation, but he does not give us any assurance that chemotherapy will work.

If it were six or eight months ago, our thinking would have been quite different. At the moment, right or wrong, the conclusion we have reached is that I should commence the chemotherapy, but obviously we are looking for something to counterbalance its effects.

Master Ni: Practically, fasting is a mild type of chemotherapy that awakens your own physical energy to tackle the problem. They cannot keep cutting parts out. Chemotherapy is very limited, but at least you know you have tried something.

*Husband: My sense is that they do not expect the chemo-
therapy to do anything except arrest the spread of the cancer.
As far as the cure, I recognize that I am the only one who
can do that. But at the moment, the serious situation appears to be to stop the spread, which seems to be moving very
rapidly and seems to be life-threatening.*

Master Ni: I understand. They will recommend the best
therapy they have to give to you, but I do not trust it a
hundred percent. I would ask you to gently, subtly pray to
yourself and ask how you can overcome this problem. The
prayer should have two aspects: First, if the problem is
overcomeable, then overcome it to enjoy the rest of your
life. Second, if you cannot overcome it, then you need to
gather your courage and with confidence say, "In my whole
life, I did nothing to harm people. My soul is pure, and
whatever happened to me physically did not happen to
my soul."

When you prepare yourself psychologically, that can
help you physically. If you keep worrying and waiting to
see what medicine can do for you, it weakens your spirit.
There are no miracles in the physical world, only in the
spiritual world. You will keep your spirit strong by getting
rid of the general level of thoughts people tend to have.

*Wife: It is interesting to me that my husband had no dis-
comfort in his abdomen until the doctor told him that the
cancer was spreading.*

Master Ni: Once told, the trouble develops faster from fear.

Husband: That also occurred to me.

*Wife: He was feeling fine, then some doctor told him, in
essence, "You are a statistic and this is what the statistic
says."*

*Now, I do not happen to believe in statistics. The problem
here is for a person who believes in statistics and is affected*

*by the man sitting across the table with all of his knowledge
and prestige, to make the leap to finding a belief in something else.*

*I wish somebody somehow would get his mind quiet
enough to see that there is more to a human being than the
body and what is coming into his head from television, news-
papers and his clients. That would be the best treatment he
could take.*

Master Ni: Right. My friend, you do not need to trust the
authorities in this matter. They are not authorities, they just
guess. If the same thing happened to them, they would be
just as ignorant about it as you are.

*Husband: I can believe that, but there are two separate things
at work here. One is the extent to which one accepts the
medical profession, and the other is what to do if one does
not accept their opinions.*

*The question is, how much does one recognize the need
to cure himself? I recognize that they cannot cure it, but I
still have passed over the question of whether the chemotherapy at this moment in time has to be accepted.*

Master Ni: There are two steps you must take. The first is
to realize that people have souls, and souls can change
houses, by this I mean change bodies, just like we change
clothes. You do not have to rely on this old clothing. First
you need to gather your life energy by giving up worldly
pursuits and staying quietly at home.

Second, our life spirit is much more knowledgeable
than we are. It knows how long we can live and what we
need to do to get better. It does not need chemotherapy,
but it appreciates your taking good care of your life. If
your spirit already knows that chemotherapy will not help,
why bother trying? You will just suffer from another expensive toy of modern medicine.

Life is independent; it is even independent of the physical
body. If you do not know that, then you will put all your

trust into what this doctor or that doctor says. If some people are treated with chemotherapy and live, it is because they were not destined to be finished at that moment. It is not to the credit of the doctors. The credit is internal.

If you turn to external authorities, it will not work. If it is a person's time to be born, he will be born. If he was born to die young, he will die young. If he is born to live to a certain age, that will happen. If in the plan of his life there is difficulty, then there will be difficulty. However, that is still talking about what is external, not internal. Internal spirit is like sunshine; even if it is covered by clouds, the sun is still there. It takes some training to experience this, but at least you can understand it.

Only you can decide what road you are going to take. The natural way will keep your soul from suffering or going through all the trouble of many doctors, injections and pain before you go away. It is not pleasant. I hope that is not the case. I think you can still be hopeful, once you decide to be hopeful.

Do they say that if you take the chemotherapy that your life will improve or they can lengthen your years?

Husband: No, they are not quite saying that. They are saying that in a certain number of cases they are able to arrest the rapid progression of the disease and that short of that, statistically and historically, it will continue to move rapidly. They don't give any period of time. So it seems to me that to add one more bad element to the seventy-three years that I put into getting where I am now in order to start something new does not seem to be so terrible.

Master Ni: I understand. Whether or not you accept the chemotherapy or whatever they suggest, I am just saying that you can make yourself strong enough to take care of anything. Cancer is one problem, but chemotherapy is another problem. You already have one problem. Isn't that enough? But you think, "Okay, I can handle two problems."

Husband: Yes, I guess I am thinking that way.

Master Ni: I would like to give you a simple example. In China, people do not have the money to pay for modern medicine. If they have cancer, they simply recognize that it is their time and they prepare themselves to go. They stop eating and stop all social excitement. They withdraw and start doing breathing exercises, drinking juice and so forth. After some time, you know what happens? They get better. Many cases like this are known to me, and this is why I recommend these things to you. I am saying that life itself can take care of your trouble. Modern medicine does not have the power to decide your life and death.

Husband: Interestingly enough, there is one fairly well known American doctor who says the same thing. He says that once you change your attitude, you can overcome the effect of the cancer. I am prepared to do that, I would just like to buy enough time to be able to do it.

Wife: I think that for me the question is not whether or not he has chemotherapy. It is what you believe in that works for you, right? My husband has already made the choice to have chemotherapy. I feel we should go from there to see what help we can give him.

Master Ni: I am simply saying, "My friend, still rely on yourself, do not think that those doctors can help you. Do not think that the chemotherapy can help you, but do take it if you have decided to do it."

Husband: I'm not sure I agree with that. I think that if I am taking it, I have to believe it is helping me; otherwise it will not help me.

Master Ni: No. Giving you something to eat to help your energy is helpful because it adds something. The new energy growing back is still your own life function.

However, if something is poisonous or half-poisonous, like chemotherapy, it only works as a purification. You can only trust that it purifies the poison. You cannot trust that it gives you any new energy. External medicine is like hiring a guard to sit at your door. He cannot increase your wealth, he can only guard it.

Husband: But I do have to believe that my own inner strength and my state of mind will make it possible for the chemotherapy to do what it is intended to do, which is to arrest the progression.

Master Ni: My friend, one thing I would like to mention is the level of the mind. Your mind needs to cooperate with your spirit, because the spirit has higher knowledge than your mind.

We over-trust the part of our mind that is formed by our education, what we heard from friends and the information we have gathered from the world, but our body spirit is smarter than our mind: it doesn't need to learn anything, because it already knows whether chemotherapy will be beneficial or not. Chemotherapy is beneficial to some people, but not to others.

I would just like for you to stay objective and be able to say, "Okay, I will do whatever is good for me, but mainly I need to rely on myself. Can I let my mind stand aside and let my spirit take the lead?"

Try any medicine you like, but always return to the center of life. That is something you brought into your life. You only need to depend on that little something for everything to function well. Once the body spirit knows itself, it knows whatever happens to you. It even knows more about it than you. But we always fight it with our mind, because we believe that worldly things can be handled by the mind alone.

We suffer much hardship because of following our mind instead of our spirit. A barber shop can help your external appearance, but it cannot improve the true beauty of your physical existence and the being within. Right now you need to prepare yourself to sit in the barber chair. Can you do that?

Life is so precious, but the root of life is not physical. The body is a partner in this short span of life. Life is something more important.

Wife: The doctor never mentioned his state of mind.

Husband: No, he didn't.

Master Ni: I realize that. Most doctors treat you like a car that needs repair.

Husband: I think that everything you say is right, but I do not see any alternative at this time.

Master Ni: The choice is yours, but you need to say that whatever you do, you will make yourself spiritually strong and not think that they have authority over your life. You are the only authority over your life. You are the one who can say, "I am going to live, I am going to overcome all this trouble."

Wife: You know, Master Ni, he has already told you the problem. The problem here is that he does not believe in spiritual life.

Master Ni: I think that is because his mind is still strong. Once it is weaker, he will see it. He will see his spirit.

Wife: How are we going to help him do that?

Master Ni: It is difficult. Usually only people who are going to die see ghosts and spirits, because their mind finally lets go of its iron grip. Sometimes people who are physically weak see the spiritual world very clearly. Strong people never see or believe in ghosts until their dying moment.

Husband: In terms of living a spiritual life, I think I come a lot closer to it than a lot of people who profess to be spiritual.

Master Ni: Yes, yes, that is true. Mainly you need to recognize the subtle understanding that you have a spiritual self and that generally it works with you.

Before I came to the United States, a Mr. Koo, Yun-che, came to me to learn the spiritual practices of my tradition. Just last year, when he was in his 70s, he spiritually knew that he needed to choose how to pass away, so he started cultivating himself seriously. For six months he ate nothing. By doing that, he cleaned himself up. He had his two sons bring him to me to confirm the final instruction for ascending. I repeated to him that if the soul exits out the top of the head, it will ascend to heaven, but if it goes through the lower part, it is bad. So he understood that matter.

Just before he passed, he called his sons and told them clearly what should be done in their lives. Then he told them everything he had attained, and those were his final words to his family. That night, he went away spiritually. After that, the body stayed in the bed for seven days. He looked asleep and in good health, and there was no bad odor. His family thought he was just having a good meditation. They were psychologically waiting for him to wake up, despite his having told them everything. When they called me to seek my instruction about what they should do to see if he was still there or not, I told them to make a soft bell-like noise, such as lightly tapping a rice bowl with a spoon, and strike it by each ear. If the soul was inside the body, it would respond and wake up.

Because there was no response, they realized that he had passed. Then they noticed that at the top of his head, there was an opening where the bone had parted and the soul had exited. That opening could be seen, even by his sons, because it was physical. The sons were happy for his true achievement.

Mr. Koo achieved himself respectably and proved the

spiritual fact that the soul is more essential than the body. He only did serious cultivation in his last few years, yet he achieved well spiritually. Before he passed away, he had small health problems, but he overcame them all through his spiritual practice. When his time came, it was his decision to go; nobody influenced him. He saw the situation with spiritual clarity.

His sons were happy that their father educated them about Tao and proved it to them by his own life. He could stay and go by his free will. I truly believe that if a person decides to manage his own life, he usually has enough energy to do it. Once you hire undeveloped people to take care of your life, it is usually not as good as taking care of it yourself.

Wife: What we are talking about here is not the mental commitment to fighting off the symptoms of the chemotherapy. What we are talking about is a kind of willingness to open up to ways of saving your life and accepting your real self.

Master Ni: In this moment, I would like you to see that you need to save your soul instead of your life. Your life is secondary, because what you think about life is that everything is here. No, everything is not here. Here is still shallow. A person can change clothes any time.

I have written a book called *Tao, the Subtle Universal Law.* You might read that book to pass the time, perhaps when you have your treatments or something.

I would also like to recommend a kind of invocation. The words are "Om kalaba, shuli hon hon." You could repeat this when nothing bothers you. Repeat it for fun. I do not say that you need to be too serious about it, but some ancient developed ones think it can wake up your soul to contact and tackle whatever problem you have. "Om kalaba, shuli, hon hon." It is only a few words, which is just the purpose, because there is no way to communicate with your own soul. Repeat it for me, please.

Husband: Om kalaba, shuli, hon hon.

Master Ni: Continue to repeat it in your mind to channel your own energy. Otherwise, you will think too much and scatter your life energy.

Husband: So far as the office is concerned, I have pretty much. . . .

Master Ni: I do not want you to have any concern about your office.

Husband: Yes, I have put it aside.

Master Ni: Put it aside and let somebody else take care of it, that is all. You do not need to worry about any external things right now.

Try to have more juice and less solid food. Solid food will support the cancer without supporting the true life substance.

Husband: Any particular kind of juice?

Master Ni: I recommend celery. Carrot or watermelon juice would also be good. Papaya is good for the stomach and intestinal problems. Any solid food will make the large intestine more burdened.

Wife: Is that also true of rice cooked a long time?

Master Ni: Later, do it later. When you cook the rice, add lots of water and cook it very long. Make it more watery than usual so it is thin, like porridge or rice soup.

Husband: Potatoes, could I eat them mashed?

Master Ni: No potatoes for you. Potatoes are too heavy for your large intestine. It is good food, but not at the time

when the large intestine does not work well. Because things
stick inside, the cancer will not be helped. At the beginning, because something was stuck there, it did not do
well; it was not clean, so it became rotten. Cancer takes
the opportunity to grow there.

Wife: You want things just to flow right through?

Master Ni: Flow through means to wash out, constantly
wash it. At the same time, the good part of the digestive
system still can take in some nutritional support.

Husband: What about things like tofu?

Master Ni: Tofu is all right, no problem. Tofu is never a
problem. Eating tofu is for the second part, not for now.

Wife: Tofu? But it is a strong protein.

Master Ni: He needs some protein. Tofu protein is usually
no harm, it is water based. The soybeans are ground into
powder, then boiled with lots of water, then condensed to
make tofu. But it is preferable to use soybean milk instead
of tofu. That is still better. You can find soy milk anywhere.
    Do the suggested vegetable juices first. Those other
things like tofu and porridge can come later. They are good
foods for all of us.

Husband: What about cooked cereals now?

Master Ni: I do not recommend cereal. If you have it, make
it like porridge, very thin, with lots of water without giving
more work to the large intestine. Also sitting too much will
cause the large intestine to work too much. That was the
source of this entire trouble.

*Wife: So he should not sit too long, but move and walk
around?*

Master Ni: Gentle movements. Several times before when I met him he walked fast, that is not helpful. Very gentle walking around the house.

Husband: I noticed that since I have been aware of the problem, there is a certain discomfort in sitting.

Master Ni: Then change it. Sometimes lie down, sometimes sit for a short time, but mostly do something and work at something. Follow this diet and if you really believe the chemotherapy will work, then do it. And read my book. Change your life attitudes. Once your attitudes change, you will be much happier within, inside. Once you have harmony inside, outside you will be happy and harmonious, too.

It is not too late, you are still strong. I would like you to be well, after that I will treat you to a good Chinese dinner. Do not be too serious about it. You will be okay.

Husband: I believe it.

Los Angeles, CA, August 26, 1989

II

Q: Master Ni, after transcribing this discussion, a few questions arose. Would you kindly answer them?

Master Ni: I do not refuse to answer anyone's question if the circumstance is right and it can benefit their spiritual growth.

Q: Why was only gentle walking recommended rather than Chi Kung exercise?

Master Ni: *Chi Kung* is *chi* practice. *Chi* is energy. People are made of energy. The *chi* can help tackle whatever problem occurs and assist in a natural way, because chemotherapy is contrary to *chi* practice, it would do more harm than good. It is almost like betting on a horse and not relying on your own inner strength any more. *Chi Kung* could be practiced when he has a better mental attitude. Then it would be more directly beneficial to his health.

Q: How would a spiritually achieved person handle such a situation?

Master Ni: When a person is dying, it is similar to a woman giving birth. At the occasion of a birth or death, there is usually a midwife, family members or friends at their side. Before the soul of the dying person has totally left the body, it sees a welcoming group of ghosts and/or achieved spiritual beings.

If the person did many bad things, he or she will have a weak spirit, and all his enemies come to surround him and take revenge. If the person's spiritual background is actually evil, the head of the demon world will come to take him away, back into the service of a demon's slave. The head of the demon world usually transforms itself into a mouse, a big fly, or an owl waiting outside in the trees: whatever does not attract other people's attention. In the case of ordinary people, the welcoming group consists of family members who have passed away before the dying person.

Spiritually achieved people will have a peaceful, quiet atmosphere. Sometimes they will experience fragrances or twilight, which may also be noticed by sensitive, living people who are present at the time. Sometimes beautiful birds (transformed spiritual beings) will come to perch on the roof or somewhere close to the house.

Without spiritual achievement, however, the soul is blocked in the body and will dissolve and scatter when the body dies. A spiritually achieved person is someone who has transformed the physical life into the subtle essence of spirit so that the achieved soul is indestructible and can exist without physical life. It is like a person who has withdrawn all the cash from his checking account. The unused checks do not need to be protected.

Sometimes the death of an influential world leader will cause a natural response, good or bad, such as storms, earthquakes, and so forth. Though there may be a strong reaction on the physical level, a natural response to the person's death is not necessarily the sign of spiritual achievement.

When an achieved person is spiritually ready, he can give up physical life in whatever way he chooses. In my tradition, there are five ways to go, which are called "untying." There is water untying, fire untying, weapon (or metal) untying, earth untying and wood untying. I think these five classifications are generalized and do not include every way. Though I think the normal way is best, in some circumstances, when spiritual people are forced to give up their physical shape, it is no trouble for them to do so.

Some achieved persons take a long time in the process of exuviation. Others can exuviate themselves quickly, like the movement of sitting down or standing up. In a brief second, the person unties his spiritual being from its bonds. The one who does it faster has subtly prepared oneself for a long time. During his lifetime, he stays or chooses a time to go, as freely as taking off a suit of clothing. This was exemplified by many achieved Zahn (Zen) masters.

Because circumstances can be different, some spiritual people give up their lives in a bad situation. This would be an event like drowning in water, burning in a fire, being killed by weapons, buried alive, hung on trees or any other violent way. Only those who know that their achievement is clear and definite, with a good worldly purpose, will submit to destruction by ignorant mortals. If they truly know what they are doing, they make the sacrifice; otherwise it brings no good to the world at all. The spiritually achieved person who has proven that his life is independent of his body in a certain sense plays a game with unachieved people who persecute him, because he knows that spiritually, his soul is intact and safe.

It is a blessing to come peacefully and go peacefully. The ancient achieved ones considered it one of five blessings: 1) general blessings in worldly life, 2) longevity with health, 3) peace, 4) wealth, and 5) a peaceful, natural death. Modern people also could achieve a peaceful, natural death, but unfortunately, they usually do not have complete knowledge about life. They allow their lives to be managed by the health industry.

Some achieved ones can transform their physical form at the last moment to be a vapor-like energy, like a rainbow light shooting into the sunshine, leaving behind only some nails and hair. In the Tang Dynasty, there was a young girl born who was interested in living a pure life. She was not highly educated, but she cultivated herself in a rural place. When she achieved herself, she took a spiritual (energy) form when she ascended. This was witnessed by villagers and local people. Many such cases are recorded. People's spiritual condition and the methods they use are different, like people who take a train or an airplane or a ship to reach their destination.

It is important during that moment, and during the seven days after the death process, because of the slow exuviation, that the body, room and environment not be touched or disturbed so as not to disturb one's concentration. No strange new energy should touch the body of the exuviating person. If you treat a body totally as a physical matter, it is disrespectful to the person.

Q: I wondered about your explanation, your discussion with the patient. We have all grown up in Western society. We have gone through the same intellectual educational system, which I myself know well. His mind already seems set on what he believes in. Do you think he will truly listen to what you have told him?

Master Ni: He is a practical person. As for the long talk at the beginning of this discussion, I do not think he picked up much. I think he only took the last part, about the suggestions for diet.

Q: Does spiritual help work only through diet?

Master Ni: In some cases, yes; diet and *Chi Kung* work. By *Chi Kung* I mean some parts of the Eight Treasures. There is also another important system of *Chi Kung,* such as "*Dao-In* of the Immortals,*"* that can help internal diseases. In a case like his, he needs to do much more than that. For example, in ancient times when people were sick, nothing was available like modern hospitals, etc. Doctors and healers were not easy to reach, so most people sought spiritual help. Because they did not really know that spiritual energy comes from the inside out, they would pray to a stone, a lake, a river, a mountain or a statue, even if it was fierce looking. They sincerely projected their internal spiritual energy outward and prayed, repented and confessed all the mistakes they had made to the spiritual image. Then, after this type of soul cleansing, if necessary they took some small measures like gentle herbs, massage or breathing exercise to bring a beneficial effect.

However, in a serious case like this, the man needs to read *The Heavenly Way* and examine himself and change his attitudes toward life. I don't think he did any bad things, but I do think he should change his attitude. For example, spiritually undeveloped people have a spirit, but their spirit is the slave of their body. A developed person makes the body work for the spirit rather than the other way around. The spirit should always be the lord of one's life.

For people today, the spiritual center is enslaved by the intellectual mind, because in modern education, the mind is over emphasized. The spiritual level is either secondary or completely ignored. When the mind plays such a dominant role, that also causes trouble.

The spirit does not care what ritual you do, what name you call it, or what picture you try to paint of it, but once

you recognize that it is your spirit, it always responds to
you and your requests. It will usually respond to you
through the same image and spiritual language you use. It
is not that it is ignorant, it is that you are ignorant. This is
how external religions work. However, it is absolutely
wrong to externalize the authority of life. In internal religions, people develop themselves enough to realize that
the external religion they follow is nothing more than a
reflection of their own internal spiritual energy.

In ancient times, people who could write would write
all their mistakes down on three pieces of paper. One would
be burned to the sky, one thrown into a river or ocean to
be carried away, and one would be buried in the earth,
asking nature to witness their change. In that way, most of
the trouble a person accumulated in his soul was cleansed,
at least at that moment. Then physically, the transition from
life to death was much easier to handle, because the physical
being follows the same law.

On a different level, it is a sign of undevelopment to
neglect learning about the body. The body can easily be
damaged if one is incapable of recognizing disharmony
within. Though it may not be easily corrected, there is a
greater chance to restore spiritual cooperation by slowing
down all mental struggles and inner conflict and offering
yourself instead to the nature of your life.

This ageless path of life that is called the Integral Way
does not bend your mind or spirit to any external authority
or false spiritual image. We bend towards the root of the
life within ourselves. If he does this, he can help himself
much more than by merely changing his diet. What happened was that the upper and lower parts of his body lost
their connection. His energy became too concentrated in
his head, and he sat for too long. So his body rebelled.

You see, the stomach is the inner room of your spirit. At
night your spirit goes down there. The bowels are the foundation of your house. If the foundation is troubled, your
house is shaken, just like in an earthquake. It is a serious
matter. However, we know that the spirit lives forever. The

body is just a house. So true spiritual development does not speed up your passing away, but turns the spiritual focus toward caring for the body. Thus *chi kung, Dao-In, t'ai chi* movement, natural medicine and diet, etc., are the tools of spiritually developed ones who take care of the house in which they live.

Even acupuncture and herbs cannot not replace the root of life within each individual. I just awaken the spiritual energy within to make a person well. It is not like modern medicine, which treats you like a worn-out piece of machinery.

If it is not too late, I think he needs subtle partners to help his earthly foundation. The only problem is that he has not nurtured the growth of his own life spirits through a spiritual practice or a natural life.

The ancient developed ones kept their mouths closed. They did not try to persuade another human being to accept their advice unless they were looking for it, because once people make up their mind, it becomes as thick as the Great Wall of China. Even though I took the time to talk with this patient, it is for him to work out himself.

Chapter 6

Assist Your Health With Acupuncture

What is popularly known as acupuncture and herbal medicine is part of a body of medical knowledge called Traditional Chinese Medicine which was developed by spiritually developed people over 5,000 years ago. It is only in the last decade that this ancient healing art and science has become a viable, respected health care alternative in the Western world. It has gained an increasing acceptance as more and more people who have not been helped by conventional medicine find integral methods of healing to be excellent tools for maintaining optimum health and preventing illness.

This brief introduction will hopefully provide a broader understanding of the full range of Taoist medicine, which I also call integral medicine.

How Does Taoist Medicine Work?

TCM is the abbreviation for Traditional Chinese Medicine. Personally, I think Taoist Constructive Medicine is a more descriptive term, because it lets you know that it is different from destructive kinds of treatment or medication.

Taoist medicine has its origin in ancient spiritual philosophy, which views a person as an energy system wherein body and mind are unified, each influencing and balancing the other. Unlike Western medicine, which attempts to isolate and treat a disease apart from the person, the emphasis in Taoist medicine is a holistic approach to the whole person.

The ancient achieved people believed that there is a universal life energy called *chi* present in every living creature. This energy is said to circulate throughout the body along specific pathways called meridians or energy channels. As long as this energy or *chi* flows freely throughout the meridians, health is maintained, but once the flow of energy becomes blocked, the system is disrupted and pain and illness occur.

Taoist Constructive Medicine uses acupuncture to stimulate certain points on the meridians in order to unblock *chi.* Western scientists have observed a variety of unique physical and electrical properties at these points, and stimulating them causes definite physiological responses in brain activity, blood chemistry, endocrine functions, blood pressure, heart rate, and immune system response.

After diagnosing a pattern of disharmony and administering an acupuncture treatment, a practitioner often writes an herbal prescription. Herbal medicine has a long history in the Orient. The first Chinese materia medica, the Herbal Classic initiated by Shen Nung during the Stone Age and completed in the latter part of the 5th Century B.C.E. Herbal formulas work to unblock trapped energy and to nourish and repair the body organs in order to cure the root cause of an illness. They also work to strengthen the immune system and help tonify and balance the entire body. There are over a thousand common herbal formulas and others that are specifically designed to treat a certain problem. A typical prescription usually consists of five to fifteen different herbs and can be taken in the form of tea or pills, as well as made into a poultice or tincture.

When the body's energy is balanced, the body can then begin to heal itself. This is why Taoist Constructive Medicine is called a natural healing method; it facilitates the body's own self-healing processes.

What Conditions Can TCM Help?

In 1979 the World Health Organization (WHO) drew up a list of diseases which acupuncture was effective in treating. These included many types of pain, the common cold, sinusitis, rhinitis, acute bronchitis, bronchial asthma, eye diseases, pharyngitis, tonsillitis, gastritis, ulcers, constipation, diarrhea, headaches (including migraines), trigeminal neuralgia, sciatica, gastrointestinal disorders, lower back pain, osteoarthritis, gynecological disorders, neurological and musculo-skeletal disorders, and more.

Most patients who have been treated by TCM notice a considerable improvement in their general health. This is because Taoist medicine utilizes a very sensitive and

complete system of diagnosis that is effective in the detection
of minor disturbances as well as serious illnesses. Thus,
treatment can be started at an early stage and often prevents
the development of a serious illness.

How much a person will be helped by acupuncture
and herbal medicine depends on several factors. These
include the nature and severity of the problem, the length
of time it has existed and the amount of physical damage
that has already occurred.

How Many Treatments are Needed?

The primary focus of TCM is correcting the underlying cause
of an illness or disease and thus producing a lasting cure.
Symptoms can often be relieved in a few hours or days,
but curing the illness itself is often a much longer process.

It is important, therefore, to take an adequate number
of treatments to ensure the best results. The number varies,
of course, with different conditions. Chronic problems
generally require more treatments than others which may
respond to a single acupuncture session. Six to ten treatments is often an average length of treatment.

Is It Painful?

Acupuncture needles are very different than hypodermic
needles that are used for injections; they are very fine and
flexible, and can barely be felt when inserted. Acupuncture needles are used to attract or disperse energy along
the meridians. They do not inject anything into the body.

Occasionally, there are some painful sensations from
the treatments, but this is caused by the mobilizing of energy
that has been stagnating and not by the needles themselves.

Are There Any Side Effects?

One of the great advantages of acupuncture and herbs is
the absence of any serious side effects. Some patients report
feeling slightly sore, light-headed, or even euphoric after

treatments. However, most people report a sense of pleasant relaxation afterward.

It is advisable to rest for at least a few moments after a treatment in order to stabilize the body. It is best not to eat a heavy meal or engage in strenuous activity of any kind right after a treatment.

Exercise/Nutrition

Throughout the long history of Chinese medicine, there have been energy enhancement exercises such as *t'ai chi movement, chi kung (chi gong)* and meditation. These are mild exercises which take little time and can be practiced daily as a curative or preventative health measure. Their goal is to integrate the physical, mental and spiritual aspects of an individual.

Chinese nutrition is a complete system of dietary principles based on traditional Chinese medicine. Its emphasis is on a balanced, flexible diet rather than rigid dietary rules.

For the past five thousand years, food and eating habits have provided the basis for maintaining health and treating diseases in the day to day life of Chinese people, and dietary therapy has proven to be the least expensive and least technologically demanding method for dealing with many chronic and disabling ailments.

The Spiritual Side

The basis of all aspects of Taoist medicine is a natural philosophy that treats the human body as a microcosm of the universe, subject to the laws of nature. Just as nature maintains a delicate but essential balance, we too must maintain a good balance in our individual lives.

My other books describe many aspects of Taoist philosophy that you may find helpful to your life and health. I feel it is important to understand the philosophy behind a healing tradition, and thus encourage you to read them.

Chapter 7

A Discussion of Eight Treasures, Chi Kung and T'ai Chi Movement

I prefer to stand up to talk to all of you, although it is less beneficial to the *chi*. When you stand, your *chi* floats up rather than staying centered. However, I believe each of you, including those who are sitting way in the back, would like to see my face and eyes to help your understanding. Better communication fulfills my obligation to tell you something, and you can better understand me.

You have just seen a performance of the Eight Treasures by the students of this center. In Chinese, this form of exercise is called *Pa Kun Dao-In*, which means the *Dao-In* exercise of the Eight Immortals. The Eight Immortals were the teachers of Prince Liu Ahn of the Han Dynasty whose book, *Wei Nang Tzu*, is one of the Taoist classics. The term *Dao-In* itself can be translated as "energy conductance."

Perhaps some of you have read the book of Chuang Tzu, which was written 2,500 years ago. It too describes *Dao-In*, which was the favorite exercise of Pan Tsu, who is believed to have lived to be 800 years old. It is not smart to ask a spiritual person how old he is. The length of a year to an achieved one can be quite different from that of most people. Pan Tsu was a minister during the reign of Emperor Niao (2356 B.C.E.). The last emperor of the Ying Dynasty (1766 - 1123 B.C.E.) tried to force him to reveal the secret of his immortality. As a result, Pan Tsu ran away.

Dao-In was developed by people who lived in caves or other remote dwellings and had to stay in one position for a long time. Inactivity stiffened their bodies and caused energy stagnation, so they needed to guide their energy flow back to normal. This is the basic purpose of *Dao-In* exercise. In ancient times, human life was much simpler, and the path of spiritual development and immortality was basically just *Dao-In*.

Today, when life is so much faster, busier and more complicated, *Dao-In* can still be used to guide confused physical and mental energy back to a normal condition.

People who do *Dao-In* generally do not need medicine; they can take care of their own health and live a very long time. The original purpose of *Dao-In* was not only to exercise the body, but as life became more complicated *Dao-In* entered a new phase that eventually developed into martial arts, from which *t'ai chi* movement developed. *T'ai chi* is only 600 to 1,000 years old, but it is different from ordinary martial arts, because it maintains the original form of *Dao-In*. Some wise teachers united martial arts with *Dao-In* movements. The *Chen* Style is more of a martial art, but the *Yang* Style is closer to *Dao-In*. Although the *Chen* Style is older than the *Yang* Style, martial arts only serve a specific type of circumstance, whereas *Dao-In* serves everyday life.

There were also movements that preceded both the *Chen* and *Yang* Styles of *t'ai chi* movement, but because most people are not acquainted with ancient movements, I cannot use them as a background to discuss my own knowledge with you.

T'ai chi movement arose out of necessity, when human life arrived at a new stage. Achieved people enjoy ancient wisdom, but they also realize the need to guard themselves, not only from attack by other people, but also from animals and other natural dangers. To effectively protect oneself, spiritual, mental and physical development are all necessary. None of them can be neglected. *T'ai chi* responded to the need for development in all three spheres of one's being.

Because the ancient developed ones, and even those of later times, knew the value of *Dao-In*, they adapted this treasure of ancient development when facing new circumstances. All *T'ai chi* students should know that it can be either a combative activity or a civilizing influence for personal development. Its use depends on the teacher. If the teacher has more cultural depth, he will place more emphasis on the *Dao-In*. People of less depth, with more achievement in the physical sphere or combat, will place the emphasis on *t'ai chi* as a martial art. As a martial art, it is certainly an excellent achievement, but martial arts are limited. *Dao-In* has a greater value because it is unlimited. I value *t'ai chi* movement as a way to adjust physical, mental and emotional stagnation. As a practice, it is a fulfillment of the cosmology of *T'ai Chi*.

I believe that most of you choose *t'ai chi* movement as a method to help your bodies and improve your health. I do not think that you use it as a fighting skill. Using *t'ai chi* as a tool to develop your life being is the direction of our wise ancestors who originally developed it. This is the traditional direction that does not come from fighting.

Today, our life activities are distributed or divided up in an extreme way. If you do physical work, usually you are physically active. When you do mental work, your mind is active. In most kinds of work, seldom can you link your mind and body together. *T'ai chi* is a special practice that can help you reunite your mind and body.

The Eight Treasures are the personal training I received from my spiritual tradition. They started with Wei Nang Tzu (206 B.C.E.-219 C.E.), whose true name was Liu Ahn. He was the grandson of the first emperor of the Han Dynasty, and he was a duke during the reign of Emperor Wu of the Han Dynasty (reign 104 B.C.E. 86 C.E.) At first, Emperor Wu greatly admired him, but he later became very jealous of him.

Liu Ahn found eight very old developed people, and they taught him the skill of spiritual self-cultivation. *Hui Nang Tzu* is the title of his book. It is a collection of the narrations written down from what the eight old men said. Their *Dao-In* practice helped them maintain their longevity. These movements were taken and reorganized as the Eight Treasures. The Eight Treasures in Chinese is called "*Pa Kun Dao-In*" (八 公 導引). *Ba Gua Dao-In,* the circle movement,[2] is different from the so-called Eight Pieces of Brocade (Refined Weaving). The Eight Pieces of Brocade is a simplification of *Dao-In* movements, but the two practices should not be confused.

---

[2] Please refer to the book and videotape of the Cosmic Tour.

The Eight Treasures preserves the original form of ancient *Dao-In*. Its sixty-four movements are a valuable tool for protecting and developing your health. It is easier for an older person to learn the Eight Treasures than to learn the more complicated movements of *t'ai chi*. A person must choose an exercise from the point of view of one's time and energy. Because of the opportunity for success and the requirements of economics, the Eight Treasures will give you a better return than a competitive style of *t'ai chi* movement.

T'ai chi movements are usually done slowly. If a healthy person, say before the age of 40, learns *t'ai chi* just to benefit his health or for a physical purpose only, its effectiveness would be hard to see. It would be easier to see the benefits of the Eight Treasures. This does not imply that *t'ai chi* is unnecessary or is less beneficial than the Eight Treasures. They are different forms of the same art. The reasons for practicing *t'ai chi*, as compared to Eight Treasures, is to augment the benefit.

Today, what people call *chi kung* (*chi gong*) is also an ancient type of *Dao-In* movement. *Chi kung* has always been popular as a healing tool in China. Many health problems can be helped by general medicine, but the personal practice of *Dao-In* or *chi kung* (different names for the same thing) has much greater effectiveness. The term *chi kung* can be translated as energy practice. It includes all kinds of internal and external practices associated with the development of *chi*, but it is different than general martial arts exercises.

The teaching of Tao values the body as a tool that can accomplish good things. Many other traditions and religions regard the body as a nuisance. Lao Tzu mentioned in the *Tao Teh Ching* that the body becomes a burden when you cannot manage it.

Some people have discovered that the human body has spiritual power. A young man called Mr. Chang put some pills in a glass bottle and sealed it. Then he sat in another room and used his spiritual power to move the pills out of the bottle. This was witnessed by a group of doctors and experts. This is not *chi kung*, it is a spiritual practice. He also performed an experiment in which many people guarded the door to an auditorium. He went in and out, but no one could see him. This was also witnessed by other people.

In another example, a woman who was a physician in the army could put a needle under her armpit, and make it break in two or more pieces. Then she could put the pieces back under her armpit, and make them whole again. Not only that, she could put a needle and thread under her armpit and make the thread go through the eye of the needle. This was witnessed by many scholars who vouched that it was true. She and her whole family had the ability to see a person's internal organs and diagnose physical problems. Many people can do that, and it is slightly beyond the general level of *chi*. That level of energy is converged higher *chi*, or *shen*, which is a spiritual power.

Many different kinds of spiritual power have been discovered and proven. Pau Po Tzu wrote about such things during the Geng Dynasty, but most of them were merely entertaining and of no practical use. There is actually a power that the human body contains; such power can be discovered and proven. Several chapters of Pau Po Tzu's book were about such things as turning water into wine and wine into water, walking on water and walking on fire. However, he pointed out that psychological and physical health and a long, natural and happy life are more important than anything else. The rest are all side effects. The main achievement is to live a good life.

Much of Lao Tzu's teaching is not understood or accepted by most people. For instance, his statements that the weak can conquer the strong, and that one who is still can surpass one who moves fast. Such things can be proven by the practice of *t'ai chi* movement. *Chi kung, t'ai chi* and push hands are not for fighting, but are an opportunity for your body, mind and spirit to connect.

Everyone breathes, but not everyone knows how to

control their breath to produce more energy. Everyone also has *chi,* but not everyone knows about it. *Chi* can be translated as breath, air or energy. It is only through certain training and cultivation that you learn about the existence of *chi,* or internal energy, in your own life being. After learning *t'ai chi,* a person could use four ounces of strength to manage a thousand pounds. This is an internal achievement that surpasses general physical strength. At the physical level alone, only a greater amount of strength can beat a lesser amount of strength, but with *t'ai chi* one learns to manage *chi* in all kinds of situations.

One important principle of *t'ai chi* movement is called "*in ching lo kung,*" which means to conduct the force of one's opponent to an empty space instead of fighting it. For example, if someone is about to attack you, you subtly and gently guide him into an empty space so that he defeats himself. This is the kind of energy management that was achieved by many famed masters of *t'ai chi.* If the movement is simple, *chi* can easily be controlled. If the movement is too complicated, it is hard for beginners to control the *chi.* This is why I recommend learning some *chi kung* in the beginning.

T'ai chi movement is only one step in learning Tao, it is not a place to stop, unless you enjoy fighting like a rooster or a bull. In my classes I first teach single, simple movements like those of the Eight Treasures. When a student achieves that, then I teach them *t'ai chi* movement. The goal of my teaching, however, is not to train people in martial arts, but to teach them the truth contained in the *Tao Teh Ching,* which is much more valuable and profound than physical movement.

To learn *t'ai chi* requires discipline. Some students may practice for several years without any apparent results, but they do not notice that now they rarely catch a cold and that other small problems have cleared up. Their whole being becomes stronger in addition to their physical strength increasing. You may not feel your energy increasing, but if you do something that decreases or hurts your energy, you immediately know it, because you feel it. For example, if you have too much sex or you play card games all night long, then the next day you will feel that you have hurt your energy. Sometimes a student of *t'ai chi* seems to be more affected by things than people who do jogging or general exercise. *T'ai chi* movement is a gentle path. It is not like going to the gym and watching your muscles develop. Ordinary physical exercise does not use your conscious mind, but with *t'ai chi* or *chi kung* you must use your conscious mind to connect each movement with the next so that when the mind moves, the body moves: both in the same direction.

The Way is simple. It is not hard to learn. It is hard to keep doing and practicing it. It is hard because sometimes the mind becomes wild and rejects simplicity. Once the mind becomes complicated, you are tempted to give up and fall back in an undeveloped stage of being. You only need to learn it right, do it right and keep doing it. It has a tremendous effect on your entire life.

T'ai chi movement involves the expansion and contraction of energy: projecting energy and collecting it. These two sides of any activity are called *yin* and *yang*. *T'ai chi* brings the two forces together in your being, like a husband and wife.

No religion can serve you better than simple, nonverbal practices. You may find some consolation from religion, but true health comes from good practices. Do not fool yourself, like a donkey following the carrot on a stick. You can put a real carrot in your hand rather than watch it hanging on a stick in front of you.

Q: Master Ni, you mentioned that a person's energy is different when he stands to speak rather than sits. Could you please tell us more about this?

Master Ni: When you stand, the energy center is higher. When you sit down, it is lower. If it is close to the natural center of the body, then it is easier to manage your energy.

If the distance between the center of energy and the body's own natural center is farther away, it makes the management of the energy a little harder.

When you are sitting, the center of energy is near the heart, which is closer to the organs of speech. When you stand, the center of energy is near the abdomen, which is farther from the organs of speech, thus making it more difficult to manage the energy and to speak well, in a refined way. Some of you are teachers, chiefs of police or managers of companies, so when you have a meeting to promote something, it is better to sit instead of standing when you talk. Learn to manage yourself before you try to manage other people or other matters. When you stand, you cannot even manage yourself well; that is how you can tell that many preachers and politicians are not saying anything truthful. Their words are floating on the emotional level rather than coming from a centered, truthful level.

Q: Can dancing be considered a kind of chi kung and can martial arts be considered a kind of dance?

Master Ni: Dancing is a human instinct; you do not need to learn it. Unfortunately, the false spiritual tradition of development suppresses the good side of instinctive dance, so many people's movements are so stiff they cannot dance. A rigid person cannot be a god, only a statue. A real god or goddess can dance, because they have the natural instinct. Good martial arts are natural acts of beauty and harmony. Though they are more serious and profound than dance, they cannot be separated from good dance.

Q: How can a person nurture chi?

Master Ni: As a Chinese proverb says: One who practices martial arts needs to keep doing it diligently; and one who wishes to learn to sing a song needs to keep singing. With any skill, perfection will come from continual, non-stop practice. So it is necessary to nurture your *chi* at each moment; you cannot forget it.

The second guideline is also expressed by a proverb that says: Of the twelve energy hours (that means a whole day and night) no moment should be separated from "this." The pronoun "this" refers to your *tan tien*, or internal center of energy or *chi*. In other words, concentrate on your internal energy centers day and night.

The third principle of nurturing *chi* is: Any thoughts you have should not go beyond what is connected with your own energy. In other words, do not daydream about things that are not relevant to your life.

The fourth principle is simplicity. Stay with only one thought or mental activity that embraces your life energy.

The fifth principle is a classic requirement of all spiritual training. There are five words given in this text on how to nurture *chi*. These five words are the foundation of *t'ai chi*: 1) poise, 2) calmness, 3) peacefulness, 4) relaxed concentration, and 5) gathering *chi*. In Chinese they are called *ding, ching, an, luh and dueh*. So when you do *t'ai chi* movement or any kind of *chi Kung*, remember these five words. First poise yourself, then calm yourself, then pacify yourself and concentrate on or observe yourself. When everything is controlled and watched by your mind, you will receive the fifth benefit, which is gain. So *ding, ching, an, luh* and *dueh* are important for everyone's learning. Follow these principles in your practice, and you will be successful. You will attain your goal without thinking. It comes simply by uniting your mind with what you are doing. The Chinese term that describes this is *chung ding*: keeping your mind on what you are doing. Most of the time, when people do things, their minds are not present. So keep your mind on what you are doing. We also call this *kuh kuh shu chung ding. Kuh kuh* means you keep your mind on what you are doing every moment. In other words, it means that what you do is observed by your own mind. Who is watching? Who is supervising? Your spirit. By so doing, you unite everything. This is the guideline from the ancient developed masters. No achieved one can depart from such a principle.

Let me tell you about another principle that is important for you to know. Can you give up all the activities that are unessential to your basic life in order to concentrate on and nurture *chi*? There were a few people who practiced such a concentrated cultivation as full time cultivation. You may ask me if I can do it. I do not, because it does not follow the principle of *t'ai chi*, which teaches alternation, like the alternation of two legs walking. Surely, I can do it all the time, but if I did it all the time, I would not have come to this meeting. I would be at home, quietly doing my own practice. I follow this principle when I doing my practice, but in much of my daily life, I follow the principle of *t'ai chi*. *T'ai chi* means alternation. When you do the practice, you need to concentrate, then after finishing the practice you do something else. That way you use what you complete in your practice to support what you are doing in your work in the world. Thus, your general life activity supports your cultivation, and your cultivation supports your life activities: writing, teaching, family life, social life and so forth.

In this tradition, the goal is to be wholly fulfilled, not just partially fulfilled like people who stay in monasteries, nunneries or caves. I do not think you can afford to lose the achievement of your cultivation by staying in a cave. Offer the beauty you have produced from your practice to other people so that they can attain the same beauty, health and power as you. Your individual achievement is not so important that you can leave behind a whole world that is weeping and suffering in continual darkness from its own mistakes. If you do not use your cultivation to assist yourself and the world, there is some doubt about your achievement.

Each person's destiny and each person's response to the challenges of life are different. All kinds of life are allowed under Heaven. That is why it is called Heaven. There is no one way that should be dominant in human life. All supportive ways are accepted. If you take care of yourself, without making trouble or being extreme, I believe that is good enough.

If there is any motivation behind my teaching, it is to continue the voice of ancient wisdom. This voice, in the future, will be planted in someone's heart: to know oneself, to nurture oneself and to improve oneself. Once everybody is better, you do not need to escape from the world to look for Heaven, because the world will be Heaven. How can the world become Heaven for you? Not by fighting bad people. It becomes Heaven when you maintain your good personality and stay away from bad people. In this way, you can become a true Buddha or *shien*. This is what I would like to share with you.

Chinese Community Center, Atlanta, Georgia
February 18, 1989

Chapter 8

Visual Energy is Connected
With Internal Movement

The traditional style of movement that we just discussed is deeply connected with personal energy: physically, mentally, emotionally, and spiritually. However, some people do not have the time or inclination to do physical arts. If you do not have the opportunity to attend a class, you can watch the videotapes I have made and benefit from them. After watching them several times, you can pick the one you enjoy most and that is most closely related to your personal energy. By watching the tape once or twice a day, the movements will call forth a response from your personal energy. Once there is spiritual response, the visual act of watching the videotape has an effect similar to actually doing the movements; it will help the circulation and transformation of your internal energy. Watching the video will produce better results if you watch it by yourself with good concentration. I don't suggest that you eat popcorn or hold hands with your loved one while you watch it! That is simply enjoying watching something with another person.

In ancient times, these movements were not done in public where other people could see them, but if someone of sincerity and good spirit keeps watching them, those spirits and that energy will be passed on to them and have a similar effect as actually doing the movement. Watching the videos will thus elevate your internal energy circulation.

The eyes have great power, but if people do not know this, they will abuse that power. One great way of spiritual communication is with the eyes. For example, in China, one highly respected art in spiritual training is calligraphy. Calligraphy has different levels. The first level is practical: everybody needs to write. On another level, calligraphy becomes art. Everyone who practices calligraphy has his or her own energy, disposition and training, so each calligraphy is different. By looking at another person's calligraphy, reading it and enjoying it, you can slowly pick up the art. If you do it yourself, you will get a spiritual response.

Practicing calligraphy for spiritual purposes is different from the level of art, however. It can be important to be able to write a talisman, for instance. However, the importance of talismans or spiritual symbols is not in the form of the letters or words but in the internal energy flow of the person writing it.

Some people who practice calligraphy live very long lives. Why? It is the concentration. Every day they spend a certain amount of time sitting quietly in concentration, doing their calligraphy.

I included four very simple and spiritually meaningful Chinese characters meaning "Peace under Heaven" in my book, *The Gentle Path of Spiritual Progress*. With continued practice in drawing them, one can also achieve a smooth energy flow and good concentration of personal spiritual energy.

Physical movement arts are similar to calligraphy. Their true importance is not the surface motions but the energy flow and internal harmony that the practitioner achieves. In ancient times, the achieved masters who were familiar with the energy route of internal movement could judge a student's progress by the depth of his or her energy rather than the outer form of the movements.

When people are young, they like to achieve something. To channel impulsive energy into worthwhile pursuits is wise. This is also the purpose of spiritual teaching. Physical movement for spiritual learning is a nonverbal practice, but nonverbal truth is always more real and direct than verbal expressions.

Therefore, if you do not have the time or opportunity to learn or practice these arts, take advantage of videos and learn at home. Their visual effect is a tool for modern people to learn spiritually. If you use it sincerely, you can benefit from it. Even when I watch the videotapes, I am almost as refreshed as if I had done the movements.

In addition to the physical movements, I also recommend seated meditation. It is also good to practice your meditation at the same time you are doing the movement. Movement

gives you one kind of benefit; being quiet and still gives
you another. Following the principle of *t'ai chi*, we should
always have an alternation of movement and stillness in
our lives. When you are still, there is movement. When
you move, there is stillness. You can also choose any single
posture in *t'ai chi* movement as a standing meditation. In
this way, you can enjoy the deep core of internal universal
movement.

When you are doing these movements, it looks like so
much movement, but practically you do nothing, because
you are doing nature. Nature is not dead stuff; it is a living
flow. Health and aliveness come from a smooth, natural
flow of energy. Thus, while nature is stillness, it is also
subtle movement. This movement starts beyond where
the five senses can reach and feel. Beyond all postures,
there is the unexpressed truth.

When we observe nature, we can see that all lives end
quickly. People are so busy following the cycle of life that
their lives are quickly over. Nonverbal *t'ai chi* movement
teaches you to experience the great truth of immortality in
each second of stillness or movement. Immortality is beyond
the cycle of life and death, death and life, enter and exit,
out and in, appearance and disappearance. It is beyond
the busy rush of the low sphere of formed life. When you
learn Tao, you learn the deep, unmoved, inexpressible
essence of the universe. Whoever reaches that can achieve
immortality in the short span of any mortal life.

You learn infinity from the limited existence of a physical formed body. You learn from doing movements with
boundaries how to reach the boundless infinity. When you
do a movement, you are in a frame of time, yet you achieve
timelessness.

Spirituality is not just reading a book or performing
rituals. Spirituality means becoming one with the infinite
truth and doing what the ultimate truth keeps doing. This
is called the Way, the Eternal Path.

Whenever your mind is scattered and you feel you need
spiritual cultivation but do not have time to learn

complicated forms, sit down and watch. Let your eyes connect with the movements in the videotape. It will calm you down, generate internal energy, and help your general energy flow. It will carry you beyond the realm of fast life and fast death. All movement is formed, yet from formed movement you reach formless eternal life. This is the value of doing the movements.

We are all equipped in this sphere of life with a body that has limbs, bones, tendons, muscles, internal organs, and nervous systems that are mortal. However, the body is also an expression of the immortal truth. When the pressures of life attract our focus externally, we forget our own truthful beings. By doing or watching movement, we can bring ourselves back from the formed external world to our truthful beings.

Do you know the secret of healing? When a person is ill, it is because energy is stuck somewhere and cannot go through one part of the body, or it has become separated from the person's life being. By doing or watching physical energy movements, you can improve your energy circulation and move through whatever blockage or imbalance you have. We talk about the power of healing, but in reality, healing is the power of being natural.

When we talk about healing power, we should also discuss the power of prayer. Many people have recovered their health through prayer, but the reason is simply that in the act of praying, energy begins to circulate again and results in well-being. What is a prayer? It is your personal energy vibration or projection. *Chi* movement is similar to prayer, but it is more calm and centered, and its benefit is greater, more practical and more scientific than any other kind of spiritual practice. Traditional Chinese medical practices such as acupuncture, herbs, acupressure, etc. all have one purpose: to move blocked energy and strengthen weak energy.

By reading my books and watching my videotapes, I hope that your life can come to a different sphere that is much broader than your present experience. It is as if you were a small fish living in a pond or aquarium. You might like to enjoy the ocean of your life. I offer many spiritual practices for reaching internal harmony. However, the most effective and economical way is to quietly watch the videos. They will help you understand the deep purpose of all self-cultivation.

Chapter 9

Guard Yourself From
The Negative Elements of Life

Traditionally, there are three fearful "demons" that stay near you, waiting to eat you up! One lives in your head, one lives in the middle of the body and one lives in the lower abdomen. They are also called the *san shihs*.

There is a special practice that was customarily observed on *Geng Shen* day in the sixty day cycle of the Chinese energy calendar. The words *"Geng Shen"* are similar in meaning to the word "renewal." On the night of *Geng Shen* day, people did not sleep, but sat in meditation and kept the three demonic energies from becoming too active. In this way, an individual would keep these energies from developing themselves and taking over his life. These deeply rooted demonic energies can become very powerful if they are not gotten rid of.

There are many other ways to eliminate demonic energy in your life, but the point is that you truly need to guard yourself from evil influences.

The first demon that lives in the high part of your body is the desire for power. Many people may not have a desire for power, but they are still bossy, assertive or tyrannical in their personal life or work. This is the power of the high "demon" that possesses you.

The second demon is the desire for possession. It is easy to develop the habit of wanting to possess this or that, with total control and complete title, so that no one else can touch it. This is especially true with regard to wealth.

The third demon in the lower part of the body is the demon of sexual fantasy or insatiable desire.

These three demons are the reason why people cannot become *shiens* or free immortal beings. A *shien* can live or both the human and the spiritual levels. For a *shien* the famental requirement is to eliminate the three demonergies that are a natural part of human nature.

gions overemphasize the negative or positive sphere

of life by personifying it, but regardless of how they are represented, people need to manage those energies. In other words, one needs to tame the strong influence of the demons and transform it into a positive spiritual support so that it cannot harm you any more.

Tao can be interpreted as a road or a middle range that cannot be traveled too far to the left or right. If you go too far to either side, you will run off the road. It is not necessary to go in an absolutely straight line, but one must stay within a middle range, with some flexibility. The size of that range depends on one's achievement. If you have no achievement, it is narrow and you can easily go out of it. If you go off of it, on one side there are trees and on the other side, there are dangerous rocks. As you achieve more, your range broadens and the road becomes wider. Then you will have a bigger range for moving left and right without moving into danger. Because these things affect your spiritual, psychological and physical health, they are important to know.

The three demons or *san shihs* are related to the three *tan tiens* or sources of vital energy: the head as the source of spiritual energy; the mind as the source of all mental activity; and the lower *tan tien* as the source of physical energy. If we took a piece of paper and wrote the three *tan tien* on one side and the three demons on the other, we could see that one side is positive and the other side is negative. Which side is stronger depends on how you live your life and conduct yourself, how you project your life energy, how you organize and manage your life, and so forth. These create positive or negative results. It is favorable to increase the positive energy and decrease the negative energy.

Again, cultivating Tao is almost like accounting; one looks for balance. It is suitable to favor the side of capital without extending oneself in debt. Overextending yourself at the emotional, mental or physical level will increase the negative side. If you correctly project your energy in all three spheres of life, then it does not cause a minus.

This method of spiritual accounting was valuable to the ancient achieved ones in conducting their lives and cultivation through the practice of self-inspection.

It was said that if a person could observe three *Geng Shen* nights each year, or in his whole life, without falling asleep and letting the hidden enemy or harm become active, then he or she would have no problems throughout life. If a person could keep *Geng Shen* night seven times, then the three demons would leave the person and let them enjoy a natural life without causing a negative result. There are at least 500 different practices to prevent harm from the three demons. It seems they are one of the more stubborn influences in human life.

Q: Do you recommend the practice of observing seven Geng Shen nights?

Master Ni: I recommend spiritual life in general.

The three demons theory has been around for at least 3000 years. Another approach to controlling the demons was through internal alchemy.

Originally, immortal medicine was totally external. Substances such as cinnabar and mercury were employed to maintain a balance inside the body. Refined metals were ingested to kill the three demons. If taken in the correct way, in the proper dosage with correct guidance, I believe they could make a disturbed mind calm down and not be influenced by the three types of desire or ambition.

However, if people treat the three demons as a superficial religious custom, it is of no use. They should learn that there are positive energies in our bodies that support us, and there are also some negative elements that should be eliminated. If we guard ourselves from the negative elements, our achievement is meaningful, not just a superstition. Unfortunately, most people do not understand that the three harms come from themselves.

There is another group of negative elements within you called the Six Greedy Thieves. They too come already

installed in your body, ready to take over y
are these Six Greedy Thieves? One of them
which become greedy for beautiful things to look at;
sometimes, this can cost you your life energy. Another is
your ears, which like to listen to sweet voices. Sometimes
this endangers your life situation. The third one is your
nostrils, which like to smell sweet fragrances and can also
cause you to sometimes be poorly poised in life. The fourth
is your tongue, which is never satisfied with ordinary healthy
food, but desires all kinds of delicious things to taste.
Overeating puts a burden on your health. The fifth thief is
your body or hands, which like to touch things that are
soft and smooth. This undermines you when it is overextended and may cause you to lose your life. The sixth thief
is the combined desires of the mind. The mind wants not
just one sensory pleasure, but all of them.

You have to be watchful that the Six Greedy Thieves do
not possess or harm you. Just remember that when your
activities stay within the middle range, no harm is done.
These things are not bad in and of themselves, but if anything is done that is beyond the middle range, it is harmful.

If you need to improve your health, examine yourself
to find the cause of your weakness. Maybe it is one of the
Six Thieves. I think you can understand and accept this
with no difficulty.

There is also a third group called the Seven Bloodthirsty
Devils. These are: 1) fear, worry or anxiety, 2) sorrow,
melancholy, grief or depression, 3) shock, 4) anger, 5) dis-
like or hatred, 6) desire or liking, and 7) enjoyment or
overexcited happiness. The teaching of Tao is that these
seven emotions can cause physical weakness or death by
causing problems such as high blood pressure or cancer.
Again, I recommend staying within the middle range. The
cure and salvation is a natural, healthy life, and the joy of
spiritual transcendence.

I would like to pass on to you the most powerful mantra
in the spiritual world. You can add as many syllables as
you please. Pronounce them correctly and loudly to disperse

all evil energy. The most sacred mantra which comes from a long line of *shiens* is "ha ha."

Remember, nurture your positive spirit. I have written a whole book for you called *Nurture Your Spirit*. Please read it, but never turn it into something to be done by your unconscious without the correct understanding.

No matter what internal or external demons or devils are in your life, the best cure is to keep looking to the goodness and kindness of your own heart. No matter how obscured, that goodness is always there.

Your external "demons," by the way, are spiritual manifestations of the internal demons you have not yet learned to tame. Once you learn to tame your internal demons, the external demons also transform themselves and are no longer threatening. Do your cultivation, be the best person you can be, be happy, contribute whatever you can to other people, and enjoy the beauty of life wherever you might find it.

Any emotion or attachment or stubbornness will cause a person to lose his or her balance. I always say that balance is Tao, and I require myself, my sons, my friends and students to keep their lives in balance. In ancient times, a spiritual person watched the three demons, the Six Greedy Thieves and the Seven Bloodthirsty Devils carefully, but too often they stayed in caves and monasteries and dared not do anything for fear of arousing the thieves and demons. Consequently, they feared the normalcy of life and overextended another side of negativity.

If you are looking for the power of self-healing or natural healing, it is important to practice self-examination or self-inspection. Beware of any demons, thieves or devils that are disguised as friends that support you. This is important. If you are not clear about the function of negative elements, all attempts at self-healing will be temporary or have no result at all, or can make the trouble even worse. The highest values in life are balance and harmony. A normal life is the best doctor there is.

The Practice of Calligraphy for Spiritual Purposes

The next method I want to share with you is Chinese calligraphy. In ancient times, this was a basic training for all children. Some adults make it their whole life. In practice, calligraphy is a training in concentration. You do not need to become a great artist, but do it with spiritual purpose. Some people who are weak because of scattered energy or who are not able to organize their minds would benefit from this practice.

Buy some white paper and a new brush. You will need to soak it in lukewarm water until the brush is soft. It is usually stuck together by a glue. After soaking it in warm water for a while, put a little black ink in a small plate; dip the tip of the brush into it, and write.

The next step is what to write. I will give you four characters. You can also write them using a branch to write in sand or in dirt, or you can write them with your finger anywhere, especially when you feel discomfort. Write *tien hsa tai ping*. Chinese words are not phonetic but are symbolic pictures, so the effects of writing Chinese calligraphy involve both the right and left brain.

Once you are connected to the subtle origin, your spiritual power is much stronger. You need to practice, though. I have taught you how to exercise your spiritual authority. Now I will teach you how to confirm your spiritual growth and spiritual authority.

You should do this practice in a quiet room, with the door locked so that no one will disturb you. It is preferable to do it early in the day.

Put your right hand into the Sword Position and put your left hand in the Thunder Position. The Sword Position is made by extending the index finger and middle finger together, while holding the other two fingers with the thumb. The Thunder Position is made by curling the ring finger over the middle finger, and then curling the index finger over the ring and middle fingers. The little finger curls over the ring finger and the thumb supports the middle finger. By writing the following four characters

tai ping, you can guide your spiritual energy
it stronger, and you can also confirm your spiritual authority. You can also visualize these characters to help you enter a state of quietude when you start to do meditation.

You may do this practice over a cup of pure water, in the morning and evening, and then drink the water. If this is done for a period of time, this is helpful for spiritual purification. In ancient times, it was used to cure chronic or incurable diseases, and was said by many to bring miraculous results.

1   2   3   4

These characters can be used for similar purposes as the *T'ai Chi* Symbol, but their effect is much stronger. They are the secret code of the Big Dipper and the North Star, which are the natural strength of people on earth and have great authority over all spirits and spiritual energies. These are ordinary words, but few people know their secret. The subtle meaning of the words "There is peace under Heaven" is that peace is within your control and within your spiritual sovereignty.

The order of the words is exact. Once you enter the quietness of your body, mind and spirit, then draw the characters in the air with your right hand in the sword position. The general response of this practice is peace and quiet. The whole world quiets down with you. You should practice them and keep practicing. You need to concentrate with your eyes wide open. This practice can subtly effect change in people and circumstances.

I hope you learn this well. It can be useful. This practice involves mostly spiritual rather than physical or mental energy. Do it gently to gather energy. It will also improve your concentration and quietude.

The Five Clouds Meditation

It is important to spend from twenty minutes to two hours each day harmonizing and adjusting your internal energy. If you can balance your emotions, you will have no anger or sadness and will not be easily excited. Listen well, and I will teach you another practice.

In doing the Five Clouds Meditation, it does not matter what position you sit in, but it is important that you are not disturbed, so unhook your telephone. You can do the practice when you feel emotionally jammed. You can stop when you think that you have done enough. For heavy emotional pressure, it is suitable to do more.

In general, you can do it in the morning or evening, after a meal, especially when you feel stuffy and mixed with emotion. As you sit, you match specific colors to certain internal organs. I suggest starting with the weakest organ, but if your health is good, then begin with the heart and visualize red *chi*, or a soft red cloud that is transformed from your heart, and watch it carefully with your internal vision. After a few minutes, watch the red cloud move to the area of the stomach and gradually become yellow. This is a purely mental practice; you need to do it until there is no "me," only clouds.

From the stomach, the cloud moves up to the region of the lungs, expands to cover both lungs and becomes white. Then, after a while, the white cloud sinks down to the kidneys and bladder where it becomes dark, like the water of the North Sea: a deep, dark blue with a little gray in it. This cloud surrounds all your water organs and then moves up to the liver area, just to the right of your spleen and gall bladder, where it changes from blue-black to green. From here, you can begin the cycle over by moving the green cloud to the heart where it becomes red, and so forth.

Do this cultivation calmly and gently, following the order I have given you. Do not change the order. Water gives birth to wood, which gives birth to fire; fire gives birth to earth, and earth gives birth to metal; metal gives birth to water, and the cycle repeats itself. By your visualization, you burn off negative energy, and the internal movement of energy will harmonize your sexual energy beautifully. People are made of living energy. Someday the physical house of your soul will die, but these five clouds will be your new home that can carry you flying. The basic goal of this practice is to fortify your energy and balance yourself.[3]

Solar and Lunar Practice

I want to show you how, in the great teaching of Tao, all people, but particularly women without men or men without women, can use the great energy of the sun and moon to balance themselves.

Men sometimes have lowered sexual energy and suffer impotence because of the tension caused by intellectual or emotional struggles in their life. Impotence is a kind of weakness. Every morning, when the sun rises, stand in a place with good air, face East and breathe in the solar energy. Swallow it and send it to the lower *tan tien*, just below the navel. Even if it is cloudy, you can still do this practice, because the sun is still there. By your spiritual development, you can make the sun's energy come to you through the clouds.

The Practice of Merry-Go-Round

To do the Merry-Go-Round, you need an open piece of ground. It is a circular movement, that can be done in either a clockwise or counterclockwise direction. The circle

---

[3]For further discussion of this practice, see *The Gentle Path of Spiritual Practice*.

is usually 28 steps; it is symbolic of the twenty-eight constellations. You do not need to draw the circle on the ground, just approximate it. The circle can be a little bigger or smaller. If it is too big, your energy will be too scattered. If it is too small, your energy will be too tight. Once you start to do it, you do not need to measure it step by step. If you measure it, your relaxation and flexibility will diminish and you will not get any benefit.

Start by imagining a flying bird or a swimming fish. It does not matter which it is; the important thing is the sense of freedom in the image. You see, the sky and the ocean provide the freedom that lets you know you are a life being that can extend your energy endlessly. Never be hurried, but do it at a speed you feel comfortable with. Do it at any time. When you do it, imagine that you are in a deep, grassy meadow, wading in a stream or walking through snow, so your steps have a little obstruction or energy field.

Your main soul is in your head, but because there are meridians that connect the top of the body to the feet, the soul is connected to the earth by walking. Your arms can be spread as wide as a bird's wings, with one hand in front and one in back, or both hands in the back. There are all kinds of postures. Go in one direction, and then when you feel you have had enough, turn around and go the other way. Relax and enjoy yourself; be creative. Create the wonderful feeling of a free flying bird. Or the wonderful feeling of a small child pretending that it is a bird.

When you are doing the Merry-Go-Round, always keep moving around the circle. There are three possible ways to walk: legs not overly bent, like ordinary walking, which will keep you higher; legs bent slightly, which will put you in a middle position; and legs quite bent, which will make you lower. I believe it is preferable to be in a natural position. The lower position is for people with a martial arts purpose. If you are too high, the energy will not center as well as if you are a little seated. Centering well means to center your energy in the lower abdomen, which is called the lower *tan tien*.

In the circle movement, there are only two possibilities; one way is with the left hand inside the circle, and the other way is with the right hand inside the circle.

There is also the variable of where to position your hands and arms. I will give the postures one by one.

Continue to do each movement until you feel it is enough or until you are tired of one hand position, then change to another. Do not change too often. Each hand position stimulates the brain differently, providing a healthy stimulation to the body systems, internal organs and the brain. This has a good effect on your general health and longevity.

1. The first position is to stretch both hands out to the sides at shoulder level, palms down, and keep them open like the wings of a flying bird.

2. The second position is to put your hands some distance from the body, outstretched at the sides around 30 degrees below the horizontal. Your arms should not be totally straight; your hands are bent at the wrists with the palms facing each other and parallel to the ground.

3. The third position is to move both arms in front of your body, about 45 degrees below the horizontal. The fingers of each hand are pointing toward each other, but the centers of the palms are facing downward towards the ground.

4. The fourth position is to form each hand like a beak, putting the fingertips and the thumb together in a point, and then bending the wrist forward so that the point is aiming at the elbow and the hands are down. Then swing both of your straight arms behind your back, so that you are like a bird flying. The arms are horizontal, and about 30 degrees behind the shoulders.

5. The fifth position is to hold up your hands with the fingers pointing toward each another and the palms facing

forward. The arms are not quite fully stretched horizontally in front of the body as high as the position of the breasts, elbows pointing out.

6. The sixth position is to raise your hands, from the fifth position, to about 45 to 60 degrees above the horizontal. This is basically the fifth position, but with your hands almost raised over your head.

7. The seventh position is to totally raise the hands above the head, with the palms facing the sky. This is the same as the sixth position, but with the arms straightened.

8. The eighth position is to hold the arm inside the circle in front of the center of the chest, with the hand bent upward at the wrist so that the thumb is towards you, and the fingers are pointing to the sky. The arm outside the circle is behind you, with the thumb toward your back and the fingers pointing toward the sky like a willow palm. The arm should be straight, but not stiff.

9. The ninth position is to point the palm of the hand inside the circle toward the center, and to raise the hand on the outside of the circle over the head, with its palm facing the sky. The arm inside the circle should have the palm facing the center of the circle, while the arm outside the circle is directly over the top of the head with the palm facing the sky.

10. The tenth position is to hold both hands in front of the body, with the elbows bent, at shoulder level, with the palms facing one another about four inches apart, but with one hand slightly in front of the other. On both hands, the fingertips face the sky. You can switch which hand is in front of the other.

11. The eleventh position is to raise the arms in front of you, with the palms open as if you were about to receive

some energy from Heaven. The palms face each other, with the arms slanted away from the body, about 30 degrees above the horizontal.

These are the basic eleven hand and arm variations.[4] You can also move along the circle by changing direction from clockwise to counterclockwise. These are a little complicated to describe. I think whatever graceful, natural way you find to change directions is best. In ancient times, these turns were programmed to be either simple or complicated, but the foundation is to make a turn, so use your creativity and see what graceful ways you can do this.

This exercise of the Merry-Go-Round is suitable to do in the morning, evening or any other time of the day, outside in the fresh air. You can enjoy doing it, and usually it is beneficial. I consider the Merry-Go-Round more natural and effective than the much more complicated movements of *t'ai chi* exercise. It is one of my favorite movements.

If the ground you use is a strip, or you prefer to move in a straight line, perhaps by moving back and forth along a private road or a road with no cars driving along it, this is called "Joyful Roaming."

If you choose to stand with the same postures, you may stand for 5 minutes to one hour. This is called "Happy Stations," or standing meditation. All three ways compose and nourish the complete system. I believe I have received some benefit from this; but at the least, I enjoy it emotionally very much. More details may be given in a later book, if I have time to write it.[5]

This movement was revised in China as a martial art called *ba gua* that is equal in popularity to *t'ai chi* movement. Like *t'ai chi* if done too slowly and too softly, or without concentration, this practice can become a sedative.

I have made a book and a videotape of the Cosmic

---

[4]Additional descriptions and photographs of the Merry-Go-Round have been published in *Strength From Movement: Mastering Chi.*

[5]See *Strength From Movement: Mastering Chi,* now available.

Tour.[6] It has many movements and changes, but the variety of movement increases the pleasure. For those who do not like to learn complicated postures and movements, the Merry-Go-Round is a good tool to assist your health, morning and evening for 20 to 30 minutes. You will reward yourself by practicing this beneficial movement regularly. If you wish, you might eventually learn Cosmic Tour. However, Merry-Go-Round is sufficient for basic health and emotion.

A student provided a different format and instructions for the Merry-Go-Round based on his own understanding. They are as follows:

Position One:
Arms - stretch out to each side at shoulder level.
Hands - palms face the ground.

Position Two:
Arms - slightly bent and out to each side slightly below waist level.
Hands - bent at wrist with palms facing the ground.

Position Three:
Arms - slightly bent and in front of the body at waist level.
Hands - fingers of each hand point to each other with palms down towards ground.

Position Four:
Arms - straight and directly behind body at a height just below waist level.
Hands - join all straightened fingers together and touch with the thumb.
        - maintaining this position, bend at the wrist so fingers point back to elbow.
        - back of the hand points down as arms are placed behind the body.

---

[6]A videotape of Cosmic Tour *Ba Gua Zahn* with a descriptive booklet is expected to be available in 1997.

Position Five:
Arms - slightly bent and in front of the body at breastbone level.
Hands - fingers pointing toward one another with palms facing out.

Position Six:
Arms - same as position five, but raised until even with the top of the head.
Hands - same as position five.

Position Seven:
Arms - fully extended and raised straight over head.
Hands - palms facing up with fingers pointing toward one another.

Position Eight:
Arms - one arm to the side inside the circle and the other arm to the side outside the circle. Elbows should be slightly bent.
Hands - bent back at the wrist with the thumb side toward the body. Fingers and thumb pointing up.

Position Nine:
Arms - one arm (slightly bent) to the side inside the circle
Hands - hand inside the circle: palm facing the center of the circle with fingers up. Other hand: palm facing the sky with the fingers pointing inward.

Position Ten:
Arms - reaching in front of the body at shoulder level, both arms slightly bent, but one more so than the other so that one hand is further out front than the other. (Switch hands occasionally).
Hands - palms face one another about 4" apart, but one hand is slightly more in front.

Position Eleven:
Arms - out to each side, bent more than slightly so that the palms can face each other.
Hands - palms face upward and toward each other. Hand inside circle should be about chin level. Other hand is even with the top of the head.

When changing from clockwise to counter-clockwise, turn the advancing foot toward the center of the circle and begin the opposite direction with the following step with the movements described above.

Chapter 10

Breathing Can Reach the Soul

Master Ni: We have been friends for two or three years. In that time, I believe you have seen many changes. In the beginning, you did not understand everything in my books, but when trouble came, then you understood it.

Visitor: Yes, that's true. I have a practical question. What can I or any of us do, at this level of understanding and development, to gather and increase our spiritual essence, our spiritual energy and our strength?

Master Ni: There are two ways to go about it. You first need to subtly guide yourself, and say: in this moment, in this hour or half-hour of cultivation, I am going to nurture my spiritual essence. I have attained enough knowledge, but I did not have time to let my spirit reflect, absorb or shine upon whatever I have attained.

So first guide your mind back. If the mind has no direction, it will be wild. Once you guide your mind, then slow yourself down. If there is a small flow of thoughts, do not be carried away by them, but always return to the original blankness of mind. Because spiritual energy has no shape, it can only be nurtured by the shapeless mind. If the mind has a focus, then you formalize your spiritual image.

Yesterday, I was talking with a student about a movie called "Out on a Limb." I talked about the experience of people from outer space who come to earth. My explanation was that achieved spiritual beings can form themselves in any shape. Why were flying discs or flying saucers hardly ever seen before, and now suddenly there are sightings of round flying shapes, especially in rural areas? They are a reflection of the human mind. They formalize their vehicles to communicate with people.

The spiritual world is like a blank screen; whatever name you call it, it will respond to you by that name. Whatever shape you give it, it will respond to you in that shape. Now we have come to a stage where we worship machines, so the spiritual world responds to people as big machines that fly. When they disappear, they leave big flower-like shapes on the ground.

It is not that the spiritual world is more developed today than it was in the past. In ancient times, it could also take any form that people worshipped or recognized as a way to communicate with it.

To get back to your question, you say you would like to nurture your spiritual essence. It is not that you need to do anything; doing something is formalizing. So do not "do" it; nurture it. Stop all other action and disturbance; let the inside of the flower, the center of all the unopened petals, grow. Your spiritual essence is protected. It continues to grow until the whole flower blossoms. You need to nurture those seeds, that core, the center of the flower within; not by doing things, but by *not* doing things.

Although it is a simple thing, it is difficult for most people, because people habitually project their energy outward, but they do not know how to gather it in; they cannot do it. Spiritual cultivation is just the opposite of extending one's energy out to the world; self-cultivation is making the energy come back to stay in the center.

Visitor: I know exactly what you mean.

Master Ni: You need to guide yourself first. You need to spend a short time sitting quietly to organize yourself. Say five minutes to start with. You can gradually increase the amount of time you spend. Then pay attention. Once you experience a small flow of thoughts, you need to guide the thoughts to come back to you. If the thoughts are too disturbing, you will find it difficult to meditate. Usually small thoughts are easy to handle, but big thoughts are not. For example, when you are in love, it becomes really difficult to meditate, because you have too many thoughts of your girlfriend. Or, if you have business trouble, you may find that your mind and energy are pulled out by the business trouble. The pressure will make you keep thinking about the trouble over and over, again and again, punishing yourself. Nobody can avoid it. You need to check out, how much trouble will result? Can you afford to take it? If you cannot afford to take it, can you avoid it? If you cannot avoid it, then what do you do? You must face it.

Once one of my spiritual friends had some business trouble and was going to lose some money; how much money, he didn't know, because it involved a lawsuit. Then in his morning meditation, because he was a spiritual student, he got the message. The message was ten Chinese words that translate as: "When you face a profit, before you take it, be careful about taking it. When you face a difficulty, think it over; if it is inescapable, face it." Those were two instructions that were very clear to him. He found the solution, because he pondered finding a way out of the trouble. He finally noticed there was trouble, and it was inescapable. This message, in the form of a proverb, meant that there was trouble that could not be avoided. He knew he needed to face it; it was his fate. So he took it. But now, he was psychologically prepared, so his strength came back, and he was no longer totally occupied by the thoughts of the trouble.

If there is a big disturbance, and you cannot meditate, the first thing you should do is ask yourself, "What is the problem? Should I face it or can I escape it?" If you cannot escape it, face it; there is no other way. Even sages need to face difficulties. We should not think we rank with all the high sages, but we know that nobody is excluded from difficulty in life. If you understand this principle, you can meditate well. Do not be too ambitious and say, "I am going to sit for one hour every day for five days, and during that time no single thought will disturb me; I will have total concentration." That is too big. Two minutes, three minutes, increase to five minutes. If you reach a certain stage for five minutes, then go to 20 minutes. Many people meditate, but they cannot stop having thoughts, so most of the day, they are half in dreams. If anybody does five minutes of excellent meditation, I tell you this: the generation of energy is more than during two hours of exercise.

Visitor: I can keep the energy circulating for different periods of time. Sometimes it is a short time, sometimes a longer time; I experiment. For instance, I sit there in quiet to do my meditation, but I cannot just be quiet. It is hard. The energy just circulates, no thoughts going on. Can I circulate the energy in the midst of activity? Can it still be quiet inside?

Master Ni: Yes, if you can manage the activity without obstructing the attention.

There are many techniques for gathering and nurturing spiritual energy. The simplest is through breathing. The important thing about breathing is that when we breathe, our mind usually wanders. But during meditation, the first requirement is that our mind cannot be scattered; we must combine our deep consciousness with breathing. It is the first step in uniting the mind and body. If this cannot be done, there are many other ways to pull your donkey mind back to the manger or feeding trough.

When you sit well, make sure there is no disturbance inside or outside. First open your mouth to poof or blow away the heat you feel in your mouth. Do this several times; three are usually enough. The heat gathered from food will cause your teeth to become loose or have early gum trouble, so that should be done daily.

Then, use your gentle breathing (gentle breathing is also called gentle fire, because breath brings warmth) to guide your mind; in the beginning, you must feel you have already dissolved yourself with the entirety of nature. Your life starts from nothingness; then you are conscious of the existence of breathing. Follow your breath, never shorten it or try to lengthen it. In deep breathing, if the breath reaches the lower abdomen it will generate sexual energy. At your age, you still have strong desire, so that is not a good thing to do. If the breath becomes too shallow, then you will pant like a dog in summertime. That is not healthy.

Let your breath be natural. Do not manage it, just follow it with your attention, expanding and contracting. Take it down a little toward the stomach to help your digestion, and then bring it back up again to your windpipe.

If you have opened the windows for fresh air, and you discover that your mind is too active, then you might practice something besides the gentle breathing method. You might try the strong breathing method, which is called strong fire or complete breathing. In complete breathing, you inhale completely, then exhale; just let the air go slowly, but not suddenly. You inhale, then you feel full inside, then release it gently, and back again. Complete or strong breathing, can also be done in the open air, as one way of exercising.

Generally speaking, only during the first part of meditation is it suggested to do strong breathing. If you can already guide yourself well, you need to directly enter a better concentration. If you do only three to five minutes of cultivation, you can use gentle breathing from beginning to end, because you only have three to five minutes of meditation. If your meditation is over twenty minutes long, then do strong breathing at the beginning and gently transfer to the gentle breathing system.

When ordinary people breathe too gently, they become drowsy and feel sleepy. Once you feel more awake and alert, immediately change back to strong breathing. After you wake up, then go back to gentle breathing. When the breath is strong, then gentle, then strong, then gentle, it means that you have difficulty. When it is strong and then gentle, it means you go smoothly.

Different states will be experienced according to your physical, emotional, mental and spiritual condition at the time. After twenty or thirty minutes, even if you feel just one second of peace, you will finish your meditation in a light, happy and refreshed mood.

In the beginning, you do not need to do it too seriously. Just work on establishing the habit. In breathing methods, there is skin breathing, bone breathing, marrow breathing, whole chest breathing, single meridian breathing, yin and yang breathing, whole body breathing, sole of the feet breathing, scalp breathing, sexual harmony breathing; the whole body is a breathing system. But to start with, the general practice is just gentle breathing and strong breathing. Form a good habit of doing this daily.

It is also important to learn single nostril breathing. In the daytime, we usually use the left nostril, and at night time we use the right nostril. You can use one nostril to inhale and one nostril to exhale; that will produce spiritual power and is connected with gathering good energy.

Success in breathing and meditation can be realized after years of practice. It is not just a matter of learning it; it is a matter of achievement.

I would like to conclude this meeting with the following thought. Sexual desire is like the salty ocean: you cannot quench your thirst with it. The more you drink, the more you will want. It is a bottomless pit. Therefore, if you are clear about wanting spiritual achievement, sooner or later you have to decide not to drown yourself in the salty ocean.

Chapter 11

Revitalization Through Herbs

A Report from Dr. Maoshing Ni

Some time ago, a mother and her lovely daughter lived alone in a Chinese village. The daughter was devoted to her mother and was very beautiful. She won the adoration of every villager. However, she refused to be courted by any men because she wanted to care for her ailing mother. It was the custom for a man to win a woman's love and the approval of her family by doing some special favor for the girl. In this particular case, the daughter put out the word that if anyone could cure her mother, he would have her as his wife. A young man from another village heard of this and was deeply moved by her filial piety and virtue. He went to the mountains to pick a variety of special herbs and brought them to the sick mother. Within days she recovered from her debilitating illness. Soon the young man wed the beautiful daughter and together they lived happily ever after. This story illustrates the popularity of herbs in everyday life in China.

Shen Nung, the Father of Herbology

The spiritual and cultural focus of the ancient Chinese was the pursuit of immortality. This pursuit can be traced far back to a very remote stage of human life, before written language was developed. The development of herbology for healing purposes came from this pursuit.

About 6,000 years ago, a leader among the Chinese tribes made his mark in history as the father of herbology and agriculture. His name was Shen Nung. A compassionate and virtuous man, he devoted his life to serving people by inventing the technology of agriculture and collecting knowledge of grains and herbs. He reputedly authored the world's first herbal medicine book, the *Materia Medica*. It was not only written to help cure disease, but was also aimed at assisting individuals' pursuit of longevity and immortality, and at preventing disease. More than 360 herbs were included in this book, and were divided into three grades or qualities. The superior grade of herbs contained edible herbs that promoted health, longevity and spiritual well-being. Fascinating legends abound and are remembered to this day in China about people attaining immortality through the consumption of some of these special herbs as a food supplement. Thus, the superior grade of herbs were ranked as immortal medicine. The premium grade were edible herbs that helped to supplement the body's good functioning and alleviate sickness. The fine grade were herbs strictly used to cure disease.

The Immortals

The organized knowledge of herbs originated from the pursuit of immortality in China. The wise men who cultivated this knowledge were recognized as spiritually developed ones. It was for the practical achievement of longevity and spiritual immortality that they empowered themselves with essential knowledge and wisdom of vast diversity, and cultivated the secrets of life. They excelled in many skills, including healing, martial arts, spiritual arts, agriculture and other selfless skills. They not only did practical healing, but also advised people on spiritual matters, marriage, agriculture, government, astrology, alchemy and other natural sciences. They were usually the oldest and wisest individuals in their community, and sometimes assumed a leader's role. They made themselves available to serve the needy and the sick, and offered guidance to the confused.

The Yellow Emperor

Over a thousand years after the time of Shen Nung another famous leader, the Yellow Emperor, emerged to help unite numerous tribes into one powerful culture. The Yellow Emperor was a descendant of the immortals. He was virtuous and served the people, as did his predecessors, by making it possible for everyone to use herbs for their well being. His book, the *Yellow Emperor's Internal Classic*, which was written by him in collaboration with his court physician, became the foundation of Chinese thought and medicine.

Self-Cultivation - The Way of Life

The objective of immortal pursuit was clear: one attained spiritual enlightenment and self-mastery, maintained optimal health and lived in harmony with their personal nature and the nature of the universe. This was accomplished through a process called "self-cultivation," which included keeping one's physical body in optimal health, maintaining a clear and calm mind, cultivating an enlightened spirit, and living a life of peace and contentment by following Tao, the Natural Way. However plain and ordinary they appeared, the ancient immortals understood the workings of the universe and possessed extraordinary powers. Whoever followed their example reaped similar benefits.

Secrets to Optimal Health

Keeping the physical body in optimal health is necessary to cultivating an enlightened spirit. The body is the vehicle for the external fulfillment of one's spirit and provides nourishment and connection to the mind and the spirit. Herbal supplements have long been an essential part of self-cultivation. Using herbs to strengthen the body and keep the mind sharp, the early naturalists were able to endure laborious martial arts training, sustain themselves during harsh weather in the high mountains, perform super-human feats, and keep their minds clear and sharp through long periods of intense meditation and fasting. They also maintained strong vitality and potency even in their old age. Most impressive of all, they never seemed to age. They always looked youthful and had the skin of a new born baby. All of this was possible largely because of the beneficial effects of edible herbs. It was one of their secrets.

The specific uses of special edible herb supplements range from formulas to nourish the organs, for women to balance the hormones, to detoxify the body of accumulated harmful substances, to beautify and give an appearance of youth to the skin, to rejuvenate one's sexual energy, and to enhance various meditations and energy practices.

The Ni Family — A Direct Connection to the Source

Among the many descendants of the Yellow Emperor, one of the direct heirs to the spiritual lineage is the Ni family. Peace in life is a blessing. This peace is the first wealth one should pursue. Other secrets and much wisdom was preserved, used and passed down from generation to generation in the Ni family. Especially valuable is the collection of herbal formulas that were compiled from the family's long tradition of healing and self-cultivation. For 38 generations, the Ni family has used these formulas as traditional Chinese doctors.

The Amazing Human Body

To effectively supplement the body's mystical power of endurance, one must understand the principles behind the healing practices of the people who pursued immortality. The human body is constructed with the same complexity and intricacy as the universe. Its delicate systems function in synchrony and correspond with amazing precision, like pieces in a puzzle. Yet, it is fragile. It reacts to and always attempts to adapt to thousands of factors and elements that we contact daily in our life. Most of the time it succeeds; sometimes it does not, and illness is then the result.

Powerful built-in mechanisms in each of us normalize and balance the body. However, it cannot perform with precision in conditions of repeated stress and poor nutrition that are so often a part of our high pressure style of living. The body requires appropriate conditions and nourishment. They can be obtained through proper living and supplementing one's diet with edible herbs.

The Benefits of Food Herb Supplements

The unique actions of herbal food supplements are to 1) detoxify 2) restore and 3) enhance the body and its functions.

It is necessary to detoxify and eliminate waste from the body. Your body, like your car, is an efficient machine that performs consistently only when it is given proper care. A car needs a periodic change of oil, cooling water, and various filters to eliminate waste products that would otherwise degrade the car's performance, or worse, render the car useless.

The human body is unique. It has all the necessary elimination systems built-in, just like a self-cleaning oven. However, its built-in system gets "clogged" by chemicals and agents unfamiliar to the body or at abnormal levels that are too high for the body's elimination systems to handle. Some of these chemicals and agents are the preservatives and additives that are found in such commonplace things as almost all foods we eat today, in chlorine and contaminants in our water supply, in smog, the formaldehyde used in most carpets, the carcinogenic sprays used on fruits and vegetables, the diverse chemicals that are in the work place, and many other things in different settings. It is no wonder that respiratory and food allergies are much more prevalent now than ever in history. Why? It is because our body does not recognize or cannot handle these unfamiliar things or the quantity of pollutants to which it is exposed.

One can avoid chemically tempered foods by eating only organically grown, natural products. One can drink purified water and breathe purified air. One can avoid enclosed spaces and live away from problem areas like the neighborhood dry cleaners or factories. But even after taking these precautions, harmful chemicals and agents still manage to get into our lives and bodies when we bathe with city water, get behind the steering wheel of a car, or simply put on a pair of dyed jeans. No one is immune to the destructive side effects of our chemical inventions.

Our body will process and eliminate a certain portion of the hordes of chemicals that enter it. The rest is simply stored in the liver, lungs, kidneys, fat cells, intestines, blood stream and skin. Many chronic illnesses result from the accumulation of waste and toxins in the body that interfere with and irritate the body and its functions. Pure foods and edible herbs act to cleanse and detoxify the body on a regular basis in order to prevent illness or disruption of the body's functions and maintain optimal health.

Restoring normalcy is what the body constantly attempts to do, but sometimes it does not succeed. Besides the wide array of toxins that invade the body, many things impact the normal functioning of our organs, secretory glands and body systems. Drinking caffeinated beverages or smoking cigarettes, for example, can overstimulate the adrenal and thyroid glands and in the long run may cause hypo-functioning of these glands. Consequently, they result in obesity and fatigue. Another example of bodily imbalance is eating too much sugar, which overstimulates the pancreas as it attempts to produce enough insulin to keep up with the level of blood sugar. One may develop hypoglycemia or diabetes later as a result of this kind of abuse. Lack of sleep and rest is another contributing factor to lowered effectiveness of the immune system that may result in heart disease and deprivation of the ability to relax and heal. The edible herbs all have restoring and normalizing effects on the overall functions of the body.

Enhanced performance is a must in our high-pressure society. Seemingly, it has become less desirable or even unacceptable to be just an ordinary performer. Progress in modern life has its costs, but it is good to remember that progress is not always forward. As we speed along in our intellectual and technological pursuits, we find ourselves forced to rapidly adapt to many changes. The balancing act between home, work and pleasure becomes increasingly difficult to maintain. Edible herbs can increase vitality, energy and stamina, promote enhanced concentration and memory, and provide essential nourishment to counteract stress.

Wholeness vs. Isolation

Unlike modern science, which reduces everything to its smallest component, Chinese medicine maintains everything in its natural whole form. The major reason that drugs cause side effects in addition to benefits is the fact that they are isolated substances in chemical form. This makes them more concentrated in toxicity; they eventually achieve their results, but at the cost of other parts of the body. Nature made each thing whole with all of its parts for a good reason: balance. The wholeness of natural substances makes it possible for potentially toxic chemicals to be neutralized by other chemicals, and beneficial chemicals to be synergistically enhanced by other similar chemicals. They are all contained within a single herb. Sometimes, however, an individual substance is not enough to address the needs of the entire body. Therefore, a collective whole is necessary to accomplish this: it is done by combining herbs together as a formula. These herbal formulas are special combinations for general and specific purposes. There are presently over 5000 substances listed in the Chinese *Materia Medica*. Each of these individual herbs has potent effects on the body, but when skillfully combined with other herbs in a formula, the beneficial effects are maximized and undesired responses are neutralized.

Four Seasons Herbs

The ancient achieved ones observed that man is a microcosm of the universe. Just as the universe has cyclical patterns, so does the organism of man. Just as the hormonal system of a female body mirrors the waxing and waning of the moon and the high and low tides of the sea, we are all governed by the law of natural changes of all living things that allows for the process of birth, growth, maturation, harvest and storage. In China, the wise ones understood the necessity and meaning of adaptation in order to live a healthy, happy life. They laid down principles and correlations describing the effects of nature on man and the response of man to nature. These principles are the theories of *Yin, Yang* and the Five Elements, which describe the natural transformations of energies in the human body and the universe. Consequently, the developed ones went on to conceive herbal formulas to help human beings effectively stay attuned to nature.

One of the more powerful natural factors that affects the human organism is the change in seasons. Modern science has finally recognized the importance of the biological clock, or circadian rhythm, and its impact on the body. During different times of the day, our body goes through a predictable cycle of chemical and physical changes that affect the functions of the organs, alter our moods, and regulate our metabolism. On a larger scale, the change of seasons also corresponds to great shifts in energy that can make one more vulnerable to illness and imbalance.

There are altogether four seasons and a transitional season of Indian Summer between Summer and Fall that correspond to the Five Elements, which also describe the functional relationships among the five major organ systems of the body. When there are imbalances in the Five Elements within our body, physical and emotional difficulties may result. Special teas or food herbs are designed to balance each of the Five Elements with the human body, and can also assist in optimal adaptation to changes of each season.

Each element corresponds to a major organ pair. Each pair of organs is most affected during its corresponding season. The correlations are as follows:

Wood	Liver/Gall Bladder	Spring
Fire	Heart/Small Intestine	Summer
Earth	Spleen/Stomach	Indian Summer
Metal	Lung/Large Intestine	Autumn
Water	Kidney/Bladder	Winter

The herbal knowledge that was developed as a sideline of immortal pursuits has been preserved and is available today to help people restore their health. By living a natural healthy life, practicing arts of spiritual self-cultivation, and using natural herbs to support your physical, mental and spiritual condition, immortal life can be realized.

Tsen Chuan

Tsen Chuan was an official who attended to the royal documents of the Hsui Dynasty (589-617 C.E.). During his 103rd year, the second emperor of the new Tang Dynasty (618-906 C.E.), Emperor Tai Chung (627-650 C.E.), heard about this man of longevity. The Emperor went to see Tsen Chuan in 639 C.E., offering him quite a wealth of food and drink as a gift, and inquiring as to the herbs the old man used to increase his years. To repay the emperor's gift, Tsen Chuan responded by telling him about his good use of herbs and his personal medical books: one on pulse reading and one with pictures of acupuncture points. However, after enjoying the gift of rich food to which he was not accustomed, Tsen Chuan passed away the next year.

The same thing happened to Mr. Lee Ching Chung, a mountain herb collector of Szechuan Province, still active during the early years of Dr. Sen Yat Sen's Republic of China. General Yang Seng, a warlord of Szechuan province who made an alliance with the new government of the republic and remained in charge of that province, took an interest in longevity. He invited Mr. Lee to Chen Tu to visit him and treated him to gourmet food and strong drinks. It was not long before Mr. Lee died.

The *Tao Teh Ching* teaches us the value of constancy and a natural, simple life. A change of diet or lifestyle in old age cannot be regarded as a favor. I think this part of the knowledge of spiritual immortality and longevity is not included in general herb books.

Chapter 12

Spiritual Practice for Enhancing Health

Beloved friends, not all diseases can be cured by medicine alone. Some, in fact, do not need any medicine at all, but only the natural healing process of life itself. Life is natural, and every living being has its own healing system and power, especially a human being who has three complete spheres of energy (body, mind and spirit) which affect each other. I do not mean that one never needs the assistance of good medical care, but simply that there is something more that you can do to help cure your physical problems. It is very important to work on your emotional peace and spiritual healing power in specific circumstances such as illness, as well as for general self-fortification and well-being.

Therefore, I would like to give you a special invocation that can be read silently or aloud. This invocation reduces emotional as well as physical pain. It can help speed up one's recovery and maintain general well-being. You should always remember that the mystical power by which all miracles are brought about is your own sincerity. Sounds and words are only used for the purpose of channeling and conducting your own healing energy and the normal flow of your vital force.

Please try the following invocation. By practicing it in a serious manner, you will match the power of the greatest achieved magicians of any time in history. At the very least, you will be able to take care of your own health and emotions.

Invocation for Health and Longevity

I am strong; the sky is clear.
I am strong; the earth is stable.
I am strong; men are at peace with one another.
I am supported by the harmony of all three spheres.
All of my spiritual elements return to me.
All of my spiritual guardians accompany me.

The yin and yang of my life being are well integrated.
My life root is firm.
As I follow the path of revitalization,
    my mind and emotions become wholesomely active.
The goddess of my heart nourishes my life abundantly.
Internal chi (energy) enhances my spiritual growth,
    and all obstacles dissolve before me.
The channels of my life energy are balanced.
My natural healing power
    contributes to a long and happy life,
    so that my virtuous fulfillment in the world
    can be accomplished.
By following the subtle law and integral way of life,
I draw ever closer to the divine realm of the Subtle Origin.

Divine Source of Health and Longevity: *Jee Jee Ru Chang Sheng Da Di, Lu Ling, Che*! (Repeat 3 times - either one or both the English and Chinese should be used, as recommended.)

(Chinese)
Tien Dao Ching Ming, Di Dao An Ning, Ren Dao Shu Jing, Hun He Chien Kun; San Chai Yee Tee, Wan Shiang Tong Gen; Zao Ching Guay Ming, Shi Lei Suei Shing; Yin Yang Hua Yu, Shui Huo Liu Tong; Guay Gen Fu Ben, Long Hu Ben Teng; Shin Shen Ling Chun, Yuin Zhuan Wu Ting, Lian Jing Lian Yie, Yee Chi Cheng Zhen; Wan Muo Gong Fu, Bai Mai Tiao Yuin, Shien Chuan Shien Dan, Fu Shi Chi Jing; Shien Lu Shien Ding, Chang Yang Shien Ling, Chang Sheng Bu Lao, Guo Man Fei Sheng.

Jee Jee Ru Chang Sheng Da Di, Lu Ling, Che! (Repeat 3 times)

It is good to repeat the entire invocation three times or more, in either English or Chinese, at one sitting. If you have a specific ailment, visualize it being healed completely and your body being restored to health and wholeness. If you are not ill, then visualize yourself as completely healthy. The hands should be held together in front of the body with the right thumb in the palm of the left hand. After the reading, gently bite the teeth together 36 times, swallow the saliva three times and bring the energy down to the lower abdomen.

This invocation can be used for healing a broken heart, too. Practicing this invocation at any time will nourish your spiritual root and balance your whole life being. Through it, you will come to know that your real being is more important than repeatedly allowing a scene from the past to pass through your mind again and again. That is what makes you suffer from a broken heart instead of reaching spiritual health. It is a matter of self-robbery. You are the one that steals your own heart and abuses yourself by continuing to dwell on pain that is long past or by engaging in negative religious practices. By doing that, you are stealing the good energy that enables you to think and feel at all. To remember this and protect your life root is to stay close to the center of life.

A tape of this invocation is available from SevenStar Communications in Santa Monica.

Chapter 13

The Power of Self-Healing

There are many skills and techniques I could teach you to help you enhance your health. My personal feeling, however, is that it is not hard for a person to enhance his or her own health. What seems difficult is taking the first step, when the trouble or weakness is still small. Some people find that rushing to a doctor creates a different problem such as a trip to make or financial difficulty. Thus, few people become interested in caring for their health until they have a problem. Once a person is interested in his health, he is usually more open to learning new things. So, first you cure your trouble, then you enhance your health by exercise and a good diet. When you recover properly and naturally, then enhancement seems much easier.

Self-healing has three levels. There is trouble of the mind, trouble of the body and trouble of the spirit. Even if I give you a practice designed to help one of those levels, all levels are affected because they are connected. Although they are all connected, each part still has its specific function.

Let us start by talking about self-healing of the mind.[7] If you cannot put your mind together, there is no medicine that can help you. Medicines may stimulate certain organs, but they are not the source of your energy. Positive generating energy is given freely to everyone, yet many people do not know how to use it. It is like a great quantity of wealth being given to someone who does not know how to manage it well, and ends up being broke. All of us received positive generating energy from nature, but because we do not notice it, we do not know how to manage it.

Truthfully, it is not that we do not know how to manage this energy. Basically, we were all born the same and can all learn how to use it. Rather, the reason why so many people do not use it well is that they do not respect themselves. They believe negative things that other people tell

---

[7] Please see my other books for more in-depth information on these topics.

them about themselves, or they experience failure and their self-esteem and look down upon themselves. If you look down on yourself, do you know what happens? You create the thought, "I am no good." A person who does that might think that even nature does not treat him as well as it treats other people. This self-doubt eats away at one's life like acid.

The standard for most people is to have a mental, physical and spiritual foundation that is neither too high nor too low. Such a standard helps us make the most of our lives. Some people are born talented and some people are born disadvantaged. I think that whoever comes to listen to me or reads my books is in the mid to high range.

If you have any psychological, mental or emotional problem, the diagnosis is simple: you do not know how to manage yourself. Actually, it is not a matter of not knowing how to manage yourself, it is a matter of not liking to manage yourself. You do not think you are worth it, or you want somebody to do it for you. Thinking of yourself as unworthy is like walking with sand in your shoes. I do not think you can walk very far unless you stop and remove the sand. Some people walk and complain that they are feeling bad, but they never stop and clean out what is bothering them. Most people notice and take care of external things that need fixing, but they postpone the internal things, which then become big problems that occupy the kingdom of their lives. Physical and psychological problems are related. The mind affects the body and the body affects the mind. It is always that way.

There are two types of patients. One type is over-nourished, while the other is under-nourished. The over-nourished ones have heart problems, hypertension, high blood pressure or diabetes, for example. These people are taking in something their bodies cannot absorb or make good use of. For example, some cases of cancer are caused by taking medication or taking some nutrition that a person does not need and that the body cannot make use of.

Over-nourishment is an internal problem. Something

that is more than enough is a bad thing. Sometimes at the beginning, a person thinks indulgence is a good thing. For example, if a person lives in the world, he or she needs some financial strength and social power. However, if he has too much and he does not know how to make good use of it, it usually becomes a self-corrupting influence. If you overwater some plants, they will die. This type of patient is like an overwatered plant. Overwatering can mean an excess of any kind: food, sex, vitamins, alcohol, emotion, thinking, exercise, money, property, etc.

Now I would like to teach you a technique for cleansing your emotions, your bad energy and the clouds in your mind. This technique is for the overwatered ones. How can you tell if you are overwatered and need to use this technique? You can tell by the feeling of being upset with or about the world, or if you think that people are uncooperative. It means that things do not happen as smoothly as you expect. If I tell a person that he has too much of something, I usually get an immediate response of, "I am not overwatered, I do not have enough." This suggests that he has set up an overly strong demand for things he should not demand. He thinks, "Despite everything nature gives me or that my family gave me, I still do not have enough."

It is hard for people to see themselves clearly. Anyone can make trouble for himself in some area of life. He may be very centered and balanced in general, but pick one thing and use it incorrectly. That is still overwatering, and he should get rid of that one thing. I think overwatering is more common than underwatering. The plants living in poor soil are a different type.

This practice for overwatered people is suitable to do in the morning rather than sitting there brooding over your trouble. It is suitable to do outdoors, and is better if it is next to a tree or a natural environment. If you live in a city, you might go to a park or somewhere where the air is better. If you cannot find better air, do it in the early morning before the air becomes spoiled.

The practice consists of six words or sounds. If you remember them correctly, they will help you. First, inhale fresh oxygen to wash your brain. No one requires you to do this, it is required for your own life. Inhale deeply, then hold it for one second. Do not force it. Then when you exhale, you will make the sound. For each of the six sounds, you will do a series of six inhales and exhales, thus making a total of thirty-six breaths with the door of your eyes, nostrils, ears and pores open to let the bad energy out.

Now I will tell you about each of the six sounds. Actually, they are not really sounds or noises; they are more like movements of air through the mouth. Each sound is done six times, so altogether you inhale and exhale thirty six times each. Inhale deeply, gently, voicelessly.

The first sound to make is *hsu* or *shui*. It is like whistling without the whistle, but just do it once in a long stream of air. This sound is beneficial to the upper part of the body, the nervous system, the eyes and the liver.

The second sound to make is *hoh hoh hoh hoh hoh hoh*. Slowly force the air out, like a person who has been crying bitterly. It is a raspy, snoring kind of noise. It is an internal adjustment that lets out acidified gas. This sound is beneficial for congestion in the chest, heart, tongue or the upper middle part of the body. It is rapid blowing, like a person whose breath is choppy because he is making an internal adjustment from crying.

At this point, if you are physically weak, stop and get up, and walk around in a circle. If your body does not feel weak, then continue with the remaining sounds.

The third sound is *fuh* or *hu*. It is made by blowing air between the upper teeth and lower lip. This sound is beneficial for the mind and disperses heat in the stomach. When you do it, you exhale with a little volume, but not as vigorously as a cat's hiss.

The fourth sound is *shih* or *szzz*. This sound is beneficial for the respiratory system. You make it by blowing the air through your front teeth which are set edge to edge. Have you ever seen a cobra? When a cobra sees people, it feels endangered and raises its head and makes this sound. Actually the cobra looks scary but he is the one who is scared.

The fifth sound to make is *whoh*. This sound is produced by puffing or blowing from the mouth. It is done quickly, as if blowing out a candle. This sound benefits the lower part of the body. To do this, form your lips or mouth into a round shape, and blow the air deeply from the lower part of your body, from the anus, large and small intestines and water system.

The sixth sound to make is *shi*, which sounds like *shhh*. It is like the shhh sound you make to tell someone to be quiet, with your back teeth edge to edge, but your lips are smiling broadly. This sound takes care of all three sections, the top, middle and lower body. It takes care of stagnation from the top of your head to the soles of your feet.

You must know one thing about human life. If your body functions slow down, you accumulate air inside your body like a stuffy room. Although it is not in the medical books, there are internal pressures created by different vapors. It is important to adjust these internal vapors by inhaling and exhaling, using the six sounds to alleviate the internal pressures caused by unhealthy, stagnant vapors. Generally, the vapors inside the body are healthy and nutritious, because they can become a kind of lubrication among the organs. It also can become a formed energy which is like something between the air and the gas type of energy within your body.

This can help both types of people that I described, although it basically helps overwatered people the most. It can also provide a temporary adjustment of underwatered people in certain circumstances.

The problem of overwatering is physical, emotional and psychological. If physical, it may manifest as a heart problem, lung problem, stomach problem and so forth. For example, if you have a congested or red eye, you keep doing the sixth sound, *shhhhhhh*. If you have a problem with bleeding gums due to congestion, you might like to read the *Tao of Nutrition* or seek dietary guidance from a competent acupuncturist or Chinese doctor. Then you should do all of these sounds, especially emphasizing the sixth one, *shhhhhhh*, because it is body heat that stays in one specific location that causes the trouble. The two sounds, *szzzz* and *hsu* or *shui* can also help your gums if they bleed. Other things also help, like herb tea or teeth cleaning, as necessary.

My second suggestion is for the "poor soil" type of insufficiently nourished person whose physical condition is bad or who has just recovered from a major physical problem. This kind of person does not have a lot of energy or stamina.

Sit in a place with fresh air, in a chair, in a comfortable posture. Bend the thumbs across the palms, then fold the four fingers over it like a baby's fist. This position is called "baby fist." Place your fists on the sides or over the abdomen, and then sit and enjoy yourself like a baby that has been fed, has eliminated and been bathed, and is now clean. This is an important position. People of Tao learn everything from a baby. The baby breathes from his belly. The baby cries, but without sadness. When the baby wants to pee, it just pees. When the baby needs to poop, it just poops. But once you get a little older, you need to postpone everything, so you are unnatural. Everything in modern life makes it, more or less, impossible to be a natural being.

However, I will teach you how to be a baby again. The first thing to learn is that nothing about a baby's body is stiff or straight. Its legs and arms are always bent a little. A good position for a person to have is for everything to be relaxed, just like a baby's posture. A baby does not sit perfectly straight. Even when lying down, the baby bends a little. That is natural. This is called "baby restoration."

Be glad when you can physically restore yourself like a baby. You should also restore your internal condition to become like a baby's energy. A baby is not dualistic like we are. It does not know the difference between the world and himself. He does not know separation. If the baby is hungry, he cries wahhhhh, looking for the breast. After the breast, lying in the cradle, he sees simple colors.

So what does this mean in terms of living a life of Tao? I am not asking you to put your thumb into your mouth and sit in a corner like a beaten child. You will only wither away or destroy your life. A baby, before becoming a child, is a natural being. A baby thinks that the entire world and everything is itself. It lies there, gently breathing. When you breathe, be like a baby, because when the muscles relax, the whole body is refilled with new energy. When it inhales, it is just like inflating a ball. Up and down, you can see the belly moving, if you observe the baby.

If you do the six breaths and practice baby-like completeness, most kinds of trouble can be cured. This is the basic practice of self-healing. One for the over-watered plant type of people, and one for the under-supported, not well-developed type of plant. You might have better terms for these.

This is basically the power of self-healing. I have also written a book and made a videotape of the Merry-Go-Round and Cosmic Tour exercises. They are actually the same system of walking in a circle and making simple hand movements. By that, you receive great benefit. The background of that kind of movement is the rotation of the earth, sun and moon. The ancient developed sages were inspired by all the heavenly bodies to combine stillness and activity at the same time. It is a profound principle, and is also great fun. It is also natural and effective. Thousands of witnesses have attested to it by their own experience.

Conclusion

Now I would like to talk about the principle of renewal. As usual, I am talking about nature. Everything follows natural cycles, except perhaps when the essence of something transforms itself into something else. If there were no recycling, the universe itself would become old. As we all know from observing nature, this is not the case. The end of a cycle is not death or destruction; it is renewal. In general, people are afraid of death and invent religion or imagined punishment. Surely death is a punishment if it is not natural.

If you walk among trees, you will notice that some trees live longer than others. Each tree has its own life cycle, which is affected by its environment. No one can expect things to remain the same, and no one can avoid internal and external cycles, especially if their life is not centered. The closer something stays to its center, the less affected it is by cyclic changes.

Each day is a new day, and each minute is a new minute and a new opportunity for the renewal of life. If we do not renew ourselves, we become heavy and stagnant. Every day and every moment that we accumulate more experience and have more contact, we become more worn out mentally and physically. Only by knowing how to renew ourselves can we face the future with freshness and enthusiasm. Renewing ourselves means getting rid of contamination from various sources connected with the different levels of life. The concept of renewal is important.

Healing is mental, emotional and physical renewal; even by opening the window to breathe fresh air you renew yourself. Renewal is more relevant than holding onto something from the past. I am not even talking about the long ago past; I am talking about just a few minutes ago. Let us say that you are upset or annoyed by something. The next moment is new; the last few minutes are already ancient history.

Renewal is easy; you let nature do it for you. But you don't need to wait for nature to recycle you; it is better to renew yourselves each day and each moment rather than wait until we cannot do anything but accept the cruel fact we do not like. We should do our best to renew ourselves, including recycling our negativity.

Even the earth renews itself. The moon, the sun and the planets all renew themselves. The Big Dipper renews itself. When things become big and old, they transform themselves to become new and small. This is the process of universal evolution. The low sphere gathers high essence; it pushes the coarse material outward and gathers the high essence within. The internal always evolves higher and higher. This is the way the world makes progress. There are different cycles and patterns of movement, but the goal is always renewal. There is no such reality as the "end." Let us say that you go to see a movie, and the movie says, "The End." Just go to another cinema and see another movie. You see, movies never stop playing. Because there is no end to your emotional or recreational needs or demands, there is no end to the number of movies that are made.

Immortality is the trademark of the traditional teaching of Tao. The word immortal is the English translation of the word "人山", *shien*. In English, the word immortality is an unnatural concept. All things can be renewed, because true immortality never implies unchangeability, like a piece of metal that eternally looks the same. All life needs and wishes to continue living, but all lives go through a continual process of renewal, aging, and decay. The difference between the English and the Chinese concepts is as follows: English "immortal" means something that does not die, but Chinese "immortal" means something that has enduring life. It means evergreen, like the tall pine trees that never change color, or ever spring which connotes the freshness of new life. All those words describe one reality: renewal. Without renewal, immortality could not be real.

Now let us discuss the connection between renewal and immortality, and two specific techniques for renewal. Nobody can become a baby again, but you can do baby practice. I do not recommend that you go home and cry for your dinner. Although it can save a lot of unnecessary words, your wife or companion or friend will not understand. Let your spiritual cultivation be a time of renewal for you. That is your time to be a baby again.

I also teach the technique of Merry-Go-Round, which comes from Chuang Tzu. Chuang Tzu once told a friend: "Do you know what is the happiest thing in the world? It is fish." His friend replied, "You are not a fish; so how do you know fish are happy?" To this Chuang Tzu replied, "Then it is birds, flying in the sky." His friend then said, "You are not a bird, so how can you know that birds are happy flying?" What Chuang Tzu understood and wished to say was that, as human beings, we watch the birds flying in the sky and see freedom. We watch the fish swimming underwater and see freedom. There is something more, though, that goes deeper than swimming and flying: unobstructed movement. If we have that, we will be happy.

Birds and fish, on the other hand, must think that because human beings can walk, they have unobstructed movement.

There is also a piece that Chuang Tzu wrote called "free roaming in nature," or "free roaming in the spiritual world" or "happy roaming." It could be translated many different ways. Sometime later, developed people used that name for the Merry-Go-Round. In it, sometimes you are like a bird, sometimes like a fish, and sometimes like a human being, roaming freely and joyfully. When you have time to be a baby, it is so refreshing. In doing the Merry-Go-Round, you have to have a childlike mood in order for it to be effective.

In our lives, we also need to accept the demands of our work and the world. Only at that time do you need to be adult. As for myself, when I teach, I am 5,000 years old or maybe two million, seven hundred thousand years old. But when I meet young friends, and I am in their company, I am the same age as they are. Later, I also have time to be a baby and a child. When a person is allowed to have privacy, one can totally be a baby or a child. It is a great pressure to be in public all the time. Also, people who live together cannot always see what needs to be learned. That is because they are obstructed by not understanding that each one needs to grow independently. Certain lessons can be learned in closeness with another, but other things need to be learned at a distance. Life itself needs some space, some privacy. When people are children, they are immature, and they need a father and mother around them. When they are teenagers, the parents' advice is usually not welcome. When they are adults, they need to learn independence and self-reliance in order to develop themselves fully.

Throughout your life, however, take some time to be a baby again, again and again. I do not think you can be a baby in public, so do it when you have some time alone. I think only in nature, in seclusion in a rural place, can one be a child again.

One of my students was a calligraphy teacher. He taught for many years but became frustrated that no one in his class became achieved to even an acceptable degree and wondered if he should quit teaching. I told him not to, because a good teacher cannot expect to have many students who meet his standards. One can offer truthful teachings, but one cannot make demands on the ones who are being taught and helped.

To live in the world, everyone needs to pay a price. That price is the job you do. So when you do your job, do it well. The point of doing any job is not to win followers, to be greatly appreciated or even to be a great success; it is merely to do your job well, no matter what the response of the world. So do your job well, whatever it may be. But when you are not doing your job, and you are allowed to be yourself, be a fish. Be a bird. Be a baby, be a child. Please, do not be a burdened adult. Be natural. Be original. Be truthful. In today's world, truthfulness and naturalness are the greatest achievement, far greater than trying to put yourself in a mold or frame that someone else has made for you. It is a great achievement to be yourself without letting other people shape you into something they promote without true knowledge of life. Others may even have true knowledge of life, but my viewpoint is that it is still better to have the time to be natural.

There are so many molds in life, but the only natural requirement of life is to be natural and original. So when you are alone and you close the door, put all masks and molds on a high shelf until you go out of your door. While you are in your room, you can be a true person, a true life again.

An achieved one is a true being, because he does not accept any external standard or mold as the truth. The only truth is that there is no mold or standard, only the original. This is the secret of salvation. If you depart from your originality, your true nature, there is no salvation for you. Are you ready for this salvation? You can be free from judgement when you have that quiet time to be a baby. All judgement is external; it is not truthful.

However profound they may be, thoughts cannot replace reality. The reality of life is that you need to renew yourself, even with regard to such mundane things as going to the toilet to empty your bladder and large intestine, and then, every four hours, to put something new into you. It is even as simple as going to sleep at night. Everything you do renews you. Therefore, make renewal your spiritual goal and practice. Do not hold onto yesterday's newspaper and worry about the world economy becoming worse and worse. The world's economy renews itself, too. Every day is new; renew yourself. Do not stay in one place or one time. Nothing stays the same. Wash away all the poisons you have accumulated from your culture and religion and be a happy child.

Thank you from a happy child, Hua-Ching Ni.

Master Ni wishes for all of you to reread the Pref an additional conclusion to this book.

About Hua-Ching Ni

The author, Hua-Ching Ni, feels that it is his responsibility to ensure that people receive his message clearly and correctly, thus, he puts his lectures and classes into book form. He does this for the clear purpose of universal spiritual unity.

It will be his great happiness to see the genuine progress of all people, all societies and nations as they become one big harmonious worldly community. This is the goal that inspires him to speak and write as one way of fulfilling his personal duty. The teachings he offers people come from his own growth and attainment.

Hua-Ching Ni began his spiritual pursuit when he was quite young. Although spiritual nature is innate, learning to express it suitably and usefully requires worldly experience and a lot of training. A hard life and hard work have made him deeper and stronger, and perhaps wiser. This is the case with all people who do not yield to the negative influences of life and the world. He does not intend to establish himself as a special individual, as do people in general spiritual society, but wishes to give service. He thinks that he is just one person living on the same plane of life with the rest of humanity.

He likes to be considered a friend rather than have a formal title. In this way he enjoys the natural spiritual response between himself and others who come together in extending the ageless natural spiritual truth to all.

He is a great traveller, and never tires of going to new places. His books have been printed in different languages, having been written at the side of his professional work as a natural healer – a fully trained Traditional Chinese Medical doctor. He understands that his world mission is to awaken people of both east and west, and he supports his friends and helpers as Mentors. All work together to fulfill the world spiritual mission of this time in human history.

For Further Information

It is said that the highest essence of truth is used for examining one's own mind and body. - Chuang Tzu

Additional materials on some of the specific topics mentioned in this book are available from SevenStar Communications. All are by Hua-Ching Ni unless specified otherwise.

Breathing

Crane Style Chi Gong, by Dr. Daoshing Ni, Chapter III, Part 3: "Breathing Regulation."

Strength Through Movement: Mastering Chi, Chapter 7, "The Breath of Life"

Chi

Guide to Inner Light, Chapter 2, pages 36-50 and 98-102 contains a discussion on cultivating *chi.*

Internal Alchemy: The Natural Way to Immortality, "Concluding Instruction," for description of the movement of *chi.*

Life and Teachings of Two Immortals, Volume II: Chen Tuan, Chapter 4: "Internal Energy Conducting and Orbit Circulation."

Strength from Movement: Mastering Chi, especially Chapter 6, "The Basis of Physical Art: Chi"

Diet and Nutrition

101 Vegetarian Delights by Lily Chuang and Cathy McNease.

8,000 Years of Wisdom, Book I, Chapter 35: "Introduction to Diet," Chapter 36: "Foods in General" and Chapter 37: "The Healing Properties of Food."

Chinese Vegetarian Delights by Lily Chuang and Cathy McNease.

Integral Nutrition: Nourishing a Healthy Life.

Tao of Nutrition by Dr. Maoshing Ni and Cathy McNease.

Exercise (Chi Exercises):
Attune Your Body with Dao-In (book and videotape available).

Crane Style Chi Gong by Dr. Daoshing Ni (book and videotape available).

Eight Treasures videotape by Dr. Maoshing Ni (book forthcoming).

Harmony/Trinity T'ai Chi, two videotapes by Maoshing Ni.

Strength from Movement: Mastering Chi for information on many different types of gentle physical arts.

T'ai Chi: An Appreciation videotape.

Health and Healing:
Chinese Herbology by Dr. Maoshing Ni.

Crane Style Chi Gong, book by Dr. Daoshing Ni, Chapter 1: "Chi Gong as a Medical Therapy."

Guide to Your Total Well-Being.

Less Stress, More Happiness.

Movement Arts for Emotional Health videotape.

Self-Healing Chi Gong videotape by Maoshing Ni.

Tao, the Subtle Universal Law, Chapter 3: "The Human Body and Universal Law" and Chapter 4: "The Art of Preserving Health."

Mind
Key to Good Fortune.

Mysticism: Empowering the Spirit Within.

Strength from Movement: Mastering Chi, Chapter 8, "Mind: The Sensitive Partner"

Workbook for Spiritual Development of All People, Chapter 3: "Work to Improve the Quality of Your Mind."

Spiritual Practices

Eternal Light.

Enlightenment: Mother of Spiritual Independence, Chapter 5: "How to Use Meditation to Attain Your Enlightenment."

Gentle Path of Spiritual Progress.

Story of Two Kingdoms

Taoist View of the Universe and the Immortal Realm.

Workbook for Spiritual Development of All People.

Teachings of the Universal Way by Hua-Ching N

NEW RELEASES

The Gate to Infinity - People who have learned spiritually through years without real progress will be thoroughly guided by the important discourse in this book. Master Ni also gives his Dynamic Meditation. Editors recommend that all serious spiritual students who wish to increase their spiritual potency read this one. BGATE 0-937064-68-8 PAPERBACK 208P $13.95

The Yellow Emperor's Classic of Medicine - by Maoshing Ni, Ph.D. The *Neijing* is one of the most important classics of Taoism, as well as the highest authority on traditional Chinese medicine. Written in the form of a discourse between Yellow Emperor and his ministers, this book contains a wealth of knowledge on holistic medicine and how human life can attune itself to receive natural support. BYELLO 1-57062-080-6 PAPERBACK 316P $16.00

Self-Reliance and Constructive Change - Natural spiritual reality is independent of concept. Thus dependency upon religious convention, cultural notions and political ideals must be given up to reach full spiritual potential. The Declaration of Spiritual Independence affirms spiritual self-authority and true wisdom as the highest attainments of life. BSELF 0-937064-85-8 PAPERBACK 64P $7.00

Concourse of All Spiritual Paths - All religions, in spite of their surface difference, in their essence return to the great oneness. Hua-Ching Ni looks at what traditional religions offer us today and suggest how to go beyond differences to discover the depth of universal truth. BCONC 0-937064-61-0 PAPERBACK 184P $15.95.

Strength From Movement: Mastering Chi - by Hua-Ching Ni, Daoshing Ni and Maoshing Ni. - *Chi,* the vital power of life, can be developed and cultivated within yourself to help support your healthy, happy life. This book gives the deep reality of different useful forms of *chi* exercise and which types are best for certain types of people. Included are samples of several popular exercises. BSTRE 0-937064-73-4 PAPERBACK WITH 42 PHOTOGRAPHS 256P $16.95.

The Way, the Truth and the Light - *now available in paperback!* - Presented in light, narrative form, this inspiring story unites Eastern and Western beliefs as it chronicles a Western prophet who journeys to the East in pursuit of further spiritual guidance. BLIGH1 0-937064-56-4 PAPERBACK 232P $14.95 • BLIGH2 0-937064-67-X HARDCOVER 232P $22.95

Natural Living and the Universal Way (VHS) - *New Videotape!* - Interview of Hua-Ching Ni in the show "Asian American Focus" hosted by Lili Chu. Dialogue on common issues of everyday life and practical wisdom. VINTE 0-937064-82-3 VHS VIDEO 30 MINUTES $15.95

Movement Arts for Emotional Health (VHS) - *New Videotape!* - Interview of Hua-Ching Ni in the show "Asian-American Focus" hosted by Lili Chu. Dialogue on emotional health and energy exercise that are fundamental to health and well-being. vmove 0-937064-83-1 VHS VIDEO 30 MINUTES $15.95

PRACTICAL LIVING

The Key to Good Fortune: Refining Your Spirit - Straighten Your Way *(Tai Shan Kan Yin Pien)* and The Silent Way of Blessing *(Yin Chia Wen)* are the main guidance for a mature, healthy life. Spiritual improvement can be an integral part of realizing a Heavenly life on Earth. BKEYT 0-937064-39-4 PAPERBACK 144P $12.95

The Art of Life - The emphasis in this book is on creating harmony ~~elves~~ so that we can find it with other people and with our ~~nt.~~ BHARM 0-937064-37-8 PAPERBACK 208P $14.95

Counsel for Modern Life - Following the natural organization of the *I* ~~c~~ Hua-Ching Ni has woven inspired commentaries to each of the 64 hexagrams. Taken alone, they display an inherent wisdom which is both personal and profound. BAGEL 0-937064-50-5 PAPERBACK 256P $15.95.

8,000 Years of Wisdom, Volume I and II - This two-volume set contains a wealth of practical, down-to-earth advice given to students over a five-year period. Volume I includes 3 chapters on dietary guidance. Volume II devotes 7 chapters to sex and pregnancy topics. VOLUME I: BWIS1 0-937064-07-6 PAPERBACK 236P $12.50
• VOLUME II: BWIS2 0-937064-08-4 PAPERBACK 241P $12.50

The Time Is Now for a Better Life and a Better World - What is the purpose of personal spiritual achievement if not to serve humanity by improving the quality of life for everyone? Hua-Ching Ni offers his vision of humanity's dilemma and what can be done about it. BTIME 0-937064-63-7 PAPERBACK 136P $10.95

Spiritual Messages from a Buffalo Rider, A Man of Tao - This book is a collection of talks from Hua-Ching Ni's world tour and offers valuable insights into the interaction between a compassionate spiritual teacher and his students from many countries around the world. BSPIR 0-937064-34-3 PAPERBACK 242P $12.95

Golden Message - by Daoshing and Maoshing Ni - This book is a distillation of the teachings of the Universal Way of Life as taught by the authors' father, Hua-Ching Ni. Included is a complete program of study for students and teachers of the Way. BGOLD 0-937064-36-x PAPERBACK 160P $11.95

Moonlight in the Dark Night - This book contains wisdom on how to control emotions, including how to manage love relationships so that they do not impede one's spiritual achievement. BMOON 0-937064-44-0 PAPERBACK 168P $12.95

SPIRITUAL DEVELOPMENT

Life and Teaching of Two Immortals, Volume 1: Kou Hong - A master who achieved spiritual ascendancy in 363 A.D., Kou Hong was an achieved master in the art of alchemy. His teachings apply the Universal Way to business, politics, emotions, human relationships, health and destiny. BLIF1 0-937064-47-5 PAPERBACK 176P $12.95.

Life and Teaching of Two Immortals, Volume 2: Chen Tuan - Chen Tuan was an achieved master who was famous for the foreknowledge he attained through deep study of the *I Ching* and for his unique method of "sleeping cultivation." This book also includes important details about the microcosmic meditation and mystical instructions from the "Mother of Li Mountain." BLIF2 0-937064-48-3 PAPERBACK 192P $12.95

The Mystical Universal Mother - Hua-Ching Ni responds to the questions of his female students through the example of his mother and other historical and mythical women. He focuses on the feminine aspect of both sexes and on the natural relationship between men and women. BMYST 0-937064-45-9 PAPERBACK 240P $14.95

Eternal Light - Dedicated to Yo San Ni, a renowned healer and teacher, and father of Hua-Ching Ni. An intimate look at the lifestyle of a spiritually centered family. BETER 0-937064-38-6 PAPERBACK 208P $14.95

Quest of Soul - How to strengthen your soul, achieve spiritual liberation, and unite with the universal soul. A detailed discussion of the process of death is also included. BQUES 0-937064-26-2 PAPERBACK 152P $11.95

Nurture Your Spirits - Spirits are the foundation of our being. Hua-Ching Ni reveals the truth about "spirits" based on his personal cultivation and experience, so that you can nurture your own spirits. BNURT 0-937064-32-7 PAPERBACK 176P $12.95

Internal Alchemy: The Natural Way to Immortality - Ancient spiritually achieved ones used alchemical terminology metaphorically to disguise personal internal energy transformation. This book offers the prescriptions that help sublimate your energy. BALCH 0-937064-51-3 PAPERBACK 288P $15.95

Mysticism: Empowering the Spirit Within - "Fourteen Details for Immortal Medicine" is a chapter on meditation for women and men. Four other chapters are devoted to the study of 68 mystical diagrams, including the ones on Lao Tzu's tower. BMYST2 0-937064-46-7 PAPERBACK 200P $13.95

Internal Growth through Tao - In this volume, Hua-Ching Ni teaches about the more subtle, much deeper aspects of life. He also points out the confusion caused by some spiritual teachings and encourages students to cultivate internal growth. BINTE 0-937064-27-0 PAPERBACK 208P $13.95

Essence of Universal Spirituality - A review of world religions, revealing the harmony of their essence and helping readers enjoy the achievements of all religions without becoming confused by them. BESSE 0-937064-35-1 PAPERBACK 304P $19.95

Guide to Inner Light - Modern culture diverts our attention from our natural life being. Drawing inspiration from the experience of the ancient achieved ones, Hua-Ching Ni redirects modern people to their true source and to the meaning of life. BGUID 0-937064-30-0 PAPERBACK 192P $12.95

Stepping Stones for Spiritual Success - This volume contains practical and inspiration quotations from the traditional teachings of Tao. The societal values and personal virtues extolled here are relevant to any time or culture. BSTEP 0-937064-25-4 PAPERBACK 160P $12.95.

The Story of Two Kingdoms - The first part of this book is the metaphoric tale of the conflict between the Kingdoms of Light and Darkness. The second part details the steps to self cleansing and self confirmation. BSTOR 0-937064-24-6HARDCOVER 122P $14.50

The Gentle Path of Spiritual Progress - A companion volume to Messages of a Buffalo Rider. Hua-Ching Ni answers questions on contemporary psychology, sex, how to use the I Ching, and tells some fascinating spiritual legends! BGENT 0-937064-33-5 PAPERBACK 290P $12.95.

Footsteps of the Mystical Child - Profound examination of such issues as wisdom and spiritual evolution open new realms of understanding and personal growth. BFOOT 0-937064-11-4 PAPERBACK 166P $9.50

TIMELESS CLASSICS

The Complete Works of Lao Tzu - The *Tao Teh Ching* is one of the most widely translated and cherished works of literature. Its timeless wisdom provides a bridge to the subtle spiritual truth and aids harmonious and peaceful living. Plus the only authentic written translation of the *Hua Hu Ching*, a later work of Lao Tzu which was lost to the general public for a thousand years. BCOMP 0-937064-00-9 PAPERBACK 212P $13.95

The Book of Changes and the Unchanging Truth - Revised Edition - This version of China's timeless classic *I Ching* is heralded as the standard for modern times. A unique presentation including profound illustrative commentary and details of the book's underlying natural science and philosophy from a world-renowned expert. BBOOK 0-937064-81-5 HARDCOVER 669P $35.00

Workbook for Spiritual Development - This is a practical, hands-on approach for those devoted to spiritual achievement. Diagrams showing sitting postures, standing postures and even a sleeping cultivation. An entire section is devoted to ancient invocations. BWORK 0-937064-06-8 PAPERBACK 240P $14.95

The Esoteric Tao Teh Ching - This totally new edition offers instruction for studying the Tao Teh Ching and reveals the spiritual practices "hidden" in Lao Tzu's classic. These include in-depth techniques for advanced spiritual benefit. BESOT 0-937064-49-1 PAPERBACK 192P $13.95

The Way of Integral Life - The Universal Integral Way leads to a life of balance, health and harmony. This book includes practical suggestions for daily life, philosophical thought, esoteric insight and guidelines for those aspiring to help their lives and the world. BWAYS 0-937064-20-3 PAPERBACK 320P $14.00 • BWAYH 0-937064-21-1 HARDCOVER 320P $20.00.

Enlightenment: Mother of Spiritual Independence - The inspiring story and teachings of Hui Neng, the 6th Patriarch and father of Zen, highlight this volume. Intellectually unsophisticated, Hui Neng achieved himself to become a true spiritual revolutionary. BENLS 0-937064-19-X PAPERBACK 264P $12.50 • BENLH 0-937064-22-X HARDCOVER 264P $22.00.

Attaining Unlimited Life - Most scholars agree that Chuang Tzu produced some of the greatest literature in Chinese history. He also laid the foundation for the Universal Way. In this volume, Hua-Ching Ni draws upon his extensive training to rework the entire book of Chuang Tzu. BATTS 0-937064-18-1 PAPERBACK 467P $18.00; BATTH 0-937064-23-8 HARDCOVER $25.00

The Taoist Inner View of the Universe - This book offers a glimpse of the inner world and immortal realm known to achieved individuals and makes it understandable for students aspiring to a more complete life. BTAOI 0-937064-02-5 218P $14.95

Tao, the Subtle Universal Law - Thoughts and behavior evoke responses from the invisible net of universal energy. This book explains how self-discipline leads to harmony with the universal law. BTAOS 0-937064-01-7 PAPERBACK 208P $12.95

MUSIC AND MISCELLANEOUS

Colored Dust - Sung by Gaille. Poetry by Hua-Ching Ni. - The poetry of Hua-Ching Ni set to music creates a magical sense of transcendence through sound. 37 MINUTES ADUST CASSETTE $10.98, ADUST2 COMPACT DISC $15.95

Poster of Master Lu - Shown on cover of Workbook for Spiritual Development to be used in one's shrine. Image is of Hua-Ching Ni. PMLTP 16" x 22" $10.95

POCKET BOOKLETS

Guide to Your Total Well-Being - Simple useful practices for self-development, aid for your spiritual growth and guidance for all aspects of life. Exercise, food, sex, emotional balancing, meditation. BWELL 0-937064-78-5 PAPERBACK 48P $4.00

Progress Along the Way: Life, Service and Realization - The guiding power of human life is the association between the developed mind and the achieved soul which contains love, rationality, conscience and everlasting value. BPROG 0-937-064-79-3 PAPERBACK 64P $4.00

The Light of All Stars Illuminates the Way - Through generations of searching, various achieved ones found the best application of the Way in their lives. This booklet contains their discovery. BSTAR 0-937064-80-7 48P $4.00

Less Stress More Happiness - Helpful information for identifying and relieving stress in your life including useful techniques such as invocations, breathing and relaxation, meditation, exercise, nutrition and lifestyle balancing. BLESS 0-937064-55-06 48P $3.00

Integral Nutrition - Nutrition is an integral part of a healthy, natural life. Includes information on how to assess your basic body type, food preparation, energetic properties of food, nutrition and digestion. BNUTR 0-937064-84-X 32P $3.00

The Heavenly Way - Straighten Your Way (Tai Shan Kan Yin Pien) and The Silent Way of Blessing (Yin Chia Wen) are the main sources of inspiration for this booklet that sets the cornerstone for a mature, healthy life. BHEAV 0-937064-03-3 PAPERBACK 42P $2.50

HEALTH AND HEALING

Power of Natural Healing - This book is for anyone wanting to heal themselves or others. Methods include revitalization with acupuncture and herbs, Tai Chi, Chi Kung (Chi Gong), sound, color, movement, visualization and meditation. BHEAL 0-937064-31-9 PAPERBACK 230P $14.95

Attune Your Body with Dao-In - The ancient Taoist predecessor to Tai Chi Chuan. Performed sitting and lying down, these moves unblock stagnant energy. Includes meditations and massage for a complete integral fitness program. To be used in conjunction with the video. BDAOI 0-937065-40-8 PAPERBACK WITH PHOTO-GRAPHS 144P $14.95

101 Vegetarian Delights - by Lily Chuang and Cathy McNease - A lovely cookbook with recipes as tasty as they are healthy. Features multi-cultural recipes, appendices on Chinese herbs and edible flowers and a glossary of special foods. Over 40 illustrations. B101V 0-937064-13-0 PAPERBACK 176P $12.95

The Tao of Nutrition - by Maoshing Ni, Ph.D., with Cathy McNease, B.S., M.H. - Learn how to take control of your health with good eating. Over 100 common foods are discussed with their energetic properties and therapeutic functions listed. Food therapies for numerous common ailments are also presented. BNUTR 0-937064-66-1 PAPERBACK 214P $14.50

Chinese Vegetarian Delights - by Lily Chuang - An extraordinary collection of recipes based on principles of traditional Chinese nutrition. Meat, sugar, dairy products and fried foods are excluded. BCHIV 0-937064-13-0 PAPERBACK 104P $7.50

Chinese Herbology Made Easy - by Maoshing Ni, Ph.D. - This text provides an overview of Oriental medical theory, in-depth descriptions of each herb category, over 300 black and white photographs, extensive tables of individual herbs for easy reference and an index of pharmaceutical names. BCHIH 0-937064-12-2 PAPERBACK 202P $14.50

Crane Style Chi Gong Book - By Daoshing Ni, Ph.D. - Standing meditative exercises practiced for healing. Combines breathing techniques, movement, and mental imagery to guide the smooth flow of energy. To be used with or without the videotape. BCRAN 0-937064-10-6 SPIRAL-BOUND 55P $10.95

VIDEOTAPES

Natural Living and the Universal Way (VHS) - *New item!* - Interview of Hua-Ching Ni in the show "Asian-American Focus" hosted by Lily Chu. Dialogue on common issues of everyday life and practical wisdom. VINTE VHS VIDEO 30 MINUTES $15.95

Movement Arts for Emotional Health (VHS) - *New item!* - Interview of Hua-Ching Ni in the show "Asian-American Focus" hosted by Lily Chu. Dialogue on emotional health and energy exercise that are fundamental to health and well-being. VMOVE VHS VIDEO 30 MINUTES $15.95

Attune Your Body with Dao-In (VHS) - by Master Hua-Ching Ni. - The ancient Taoist predecessor to Tai Chi Chuan. Performed sitting and lying down, these moves unblock stagnant energy. Includes meditations and massage for a complete integral fitness program. VDAOI VHS VIDEO 60 MINUTES $39.95

T'ai Chi Ch'uan: An Appreciation (VHS) - by Hua-Ching Ni. - "Gentle Path," "Sky Journey" and "Infinite Expansion" are three Taoist esoteric styles handed down by highly achieved masters and are shown in an uninterrupted format. Not an instructional video. VAPPR VHS VIDEO 30 MINUTES $24.95

Self-Healing Chi Gong (VHS Video) - Strengthen your own self-healing powers. These effective mind-body exercises strengthen and balance each of your five major organ systems. Two hours of practical demonstrations and information lectures. VSHCG VHS VIDEO 120 MINUTES $39.95

Crane Style Chi Gong (VHS) - by Dr. Daoshing Ni, Ph.D. - These ancient exercises are practiced for healing purposes. They integrate movement, mental imagery and breathing techniques. To be used with the book. VCRAN VHS VIDEO 120 MINUTES $39.95

Taoist Eight Treasures (VHS) - By Maoshing Ni, Ph.D. - Unique to the Ni family, these 32 exercises open blocks in the energy flow and strengthen one's vitality. Combines stretching, toning and energy conducting with deep breathing. VEIGH VHS VIDEO 105 MINUTES $39.95

T'ai Chi Ch'uan I & II (VHS) - By Maoshing Ni, Ph.D. - This Taoist style, called the style of Harmony, is a distillation of the Yang, Chen and Wu styles. It integrates physical movement with internal energy and helps promote longevity and self cultivation. VTAI1 VHS VIDEO PART 1 60 MINUTES $39.95 • VTAI2 VHS VIDEO PART 2 60 MINUTES

AUDIO CASSETTES

Invocations for Health, Longevity and Healing a Broken Heart - By Maoshing Ni, Ph.D. - "Thinking is louder than thunder." This cassette guides you through a series of invocations to channel and conduct your own healing energy and vital force. AINVO AUDIO 30 MINUTES $9.95

Stress Release with Chi Gong - By Maoshing Ni, Ph.D. - This audio cassette guides you through simple breathing techniques that enable you to release stress and tension that are a common cause of illness today. ACHIS AUDIO 30 MINUTES $9.95

Pain Management with Chi Gong - By Maoshing Ni, Ph.D. - Using visualization and deep-breathing techniques, this cassette offers methods for overcoming pain by invigorating your energy flow and unblocking obstructions that cause pain. ACHIP AUDIO 30 MINUTES $9.95

Tao Teh Ching Cassette Tapes - This classic work of Lao Tzu has been recorded in this two-cassette set that is a companion to the book translated by Hua-Ching Ni. Professionally recorded and read by Robert Rudelson. ATAOT 120 MINUTES $12.95

BOOKS IN SPANISH

Tao Teh Ching - En Espanol. BSPAN 0-937064-92-0 PAPERBACK 112 P $8.95

Order Form

name _____

street address _____

city _____ state _____ zip _____

phone (day) _____ (evening) _____

best time to call _____

Credit Card Information (Visa or MasterCard Only)

Credit Card Number _____

Exp. Date _____

Signature _____

Quantity	Price	Title	5 Letter Code	Total

Sub total _____

Sales Tax (CA residents only, 8.25%) _____

Shipping (see left) _____

Total Amount Enclosed _____

Mail this form with payment
(US funds only) to:

SevenStar Communications
1314 Second Street
Santa Monica, CA 90401 USA

Credit Card Orders:
Call 1-800-578-9526
Fax 310-917-2267
E-Mail taostar@netcom.com

Others Please Call
1-310-576-1901

Shipping Charges

Number of items	Domestic		International			
	UPS Ground	4th Class Book Rate USmail	Surface USmail	Air [2] Printed Matter USmail	Air Parcel Rate USmail	UPS Int'l Air
First Item [1]	4.50	2.00	2.50	7.50	12.00	46.00
Each Additional Item	0.50	0.50	1.00	5.00 [3]	6.00	6.00

NOTES
[1] BOOK OF CHANGES (I CHING) because of weight, counts as 3 items; all other books count as 1 item each.
[2] USmail Air Printed Matter Table to be used for European destination only. All others use Air Parcel Rate.
[3] Limit of 4 items only for this service.

DELIVERY TIMES:
UPS Ground: 7 - 10 days. Insured
4th Class Book Rate USmail: 5 - 8 weeks. Uninsured
Surface USmail (Overseas): 6 - 9 weeks. Uninsured
Air Printed Matter USmail (Overseas): 2 - 4 weeks. Uninsured
Air Parcel Rate USmail: 2 - 4 weeks. Insured
UPS International Air: 4 days. Insured

SEVEN STAR COMMUNICATIONS

Spiritual Study and Teaching Through the College of Tao

The College of Tao (COT) and the Union of Tao and Man were formally established in California in the 1970's, yet this tradition is a very broad spiritual culture containing centuries of human spiritual growth. Its central goal is to offer healthy spiritual education to all people. The goal of the school is to help individuals develop themselves for a spiritually developed world. This time-tested school values the spiritual development of each individual self and passes down its guidance and experience.

COT is a school which has no walls. The big human society is its classroom. Your own life and service is the class you attend; thus students grow from their lives and from studying the guidance of the Universal Way.

Any interested individual is welcome to join and learn to grow for oneself. The Self-Study Program can be useful to you. The Program, which is based on Master Ni's books and videotapes, gives people who wish to study on their own or are too far from a volunteer teacher an opportunity to study the Way at their own speed. The outline for the Self-Study Program is in the book *The Golden Message*. If you choose, the Correspondence Course is also available.

A Mentor is any individual who is spiritually self-responsible and who sets up a model of a healthy and complete life for oneself and others. They may serve as teachers for general society and people with preliminary interest in spiritual development. To receive recognition from the USIW for teaching activity, a Mentor must first register with the USIW and follow the Mentor Service Handbook which was written by Mentors. They can teach special skills which are certified by the USIW. It is recommended that all students use the Correspondence Course or self-study program to educate themselves to be Mentors, but students also may learn directly from a Mentors. COT also offers special seminars which are taught only to Mentors.

- -

If you are interested in the Integral Way Correspondence Course/Self-Study Program, please write: College of Tao, PO Box 1222, El Prado, NM 87529.

- -

Mail to: USIW, PO Box 28993, Atlanta, GA 30358-0993

❏ I wish to be put on the mailing list of the USIW to be notified of educational activities.

❏ I wish to receive a list of Registered Mentors teaching in my area or country.

❏ I am interested in joining /forming a study group in my area.

❏ I am interested in becoming a Mentor of the USIW.

Name:_____

Address:_____

City:_____State:_____Zip:_____

Herbs Used by Ancient Masters

The pursuit of everlasting youth or immortality throughout human history is an innate human desire. Long ago, Chinese esoteric Taoists went to the high mountains to contemplate nature, strengthen their bodies, empower their minds and develop their spirit. From their studies and cultivation, they gave China alchemy and chemistry, herbology and acupuncture, the I Ching, astrology, martial arts and T'ai Chi Ch'uan, Chi Gong and many other useful kinds of knowledge.

Most important, they handed down in secrecy methods for attaining longevity and spiritual immortality. There were different levels of approach; one was to use a collection of food herb formulas that were only available to highly achieved Taoist masters. They used these food herbs to increase energy and heighten vitality. This treasured collection of herbal formulas remained within the Ni family for centuries.

Now, through Traditions of Tao, the Ni family makes these foods available for you to use to assist the foundation of your own positive development. It is only with a strong foundation that expected results are produced from diligent cultivation.

As a further benefit, in concert with the Taoist principle of self-sufficiency, Traditions of Tao offers the food herbs along with SevenStar Communication's publications in a distribution opportunity for anyone serious about financial independence.

Send to: Traditions of Tao
             1314 Second Street #200
             Santa Monica, CA 90401

Please send me a Traditions of Tao brochure.

Name _____

Address_____

City_____State_____Zip_____

Phone (day)_____(evening)_____

Yo San University of Traditional Chinese Medicine

"Not just a medical career, but a life-time commitment to raising one's spiritual standard."

Thank you for your support and interest in our publications and services. It is by your patronage that we continue to offer you the practical knowledge and wisdom from this venerable Taoist tradition.

Because of your sustained interest in natural health, in January 1989 we formed Yo San University of Traditional Chinese Medicine, a non-profit educational institution under the direction of founder Master Ni, Hua-Ching. Yo San University is the continuation of 38 generations of Ni family practitioners who handed down knowledge and wisdom from father to son. Its purpose is to train and graduate practitioners of the highest caliber in Traditional Chinese Medicine, which includes acupuncture, herbology and spiritual development.

We view Traditional Chinese Medicine as the application of spiritual development. Its foundation is the spiritual capability to know life, diagnose a person's problem and cure it. We teach students how to care for themselves and others, emphasizing the integration of traditional knowledge and modern science. Yo San University offers a complete accredited Master's degree program approved by the California State Department of Education that provides an excellent education in Traditional Chinese Medicine and meets all requirements for state licensure. Federal financial aid and scholarships are available.

We invite you to inquire into our university for a creative and rewarding career as a holistic physician. Classes are also open to persons interested only in self-enrichment. For more information, please fill out the form below and send it to:

Yo San University of Traditional Chinese Medicine
1314 Second Street
Santa Monica, CA 90401 U.S.A.

❑   Please send me information on the Masters degree program in Traditional Chinese Medicine.

❑   Please send me information on health workshops and seminars.

❑   Please send me information on continuing education for acupuncturists and health professionals.

Name _____

Address_____

City_____State_____Zip_____

Phone(day)_____(evening)_____

Index